MW00441320

ENDORSEMENTS

Who better to pattern life after than Jesus? Stephen Caldwell has unpacked the profoundly simple (yet simply profound) growth process of Jesus of Nazareth. With skill and insight he guides us on a journey — not too much detail (nor too little), no laborious checklists or exhaustive strategies — just a steady hand pointing the way after the Master.

– Dr. Robert V. Cupp
Fellowship Bible Church of Northwest Arkansas

Leaders grow. They aren't content with staying the same, because they know God always wants to draw them closer and do more with them. So if you're looking for a growth plan, the one modeled by Jesus is a great place to start.

– Brad Lomenick
Founder of BLINC, author of *H3 Leadership* and
The Catalyst Leader and former president of Catalyst

This book had me at the Preface. Within five minutes I had already taken action. Grow Like Jesus *has captured a single but powerful verse and brought it to life. Life application abounds!*

– David Roth
President, WorkMatters

There are more than 31,000 verses in the Bible. My friend Stephen Caldwell teaches us that one verse, found in the Book of Luke, sums it all up – Faith in Christ is a one-time decision that leads to a lifetime of growth. And that is exactly what this important book will do – help you Grow Like Jesus.

– Tommy Spaulding

New York Times bestselling author of *It's Not Just Who You Know* and *The Heart-Led Leader*

I have been blessed through the years to read advanced copies of books and, on occasion, to offer an endorsement. When I started Stephen's book, Grow Like Jesus, based on one verse of scripture, I was intrigued. As I read it, I was encouraged, challenged and inspired. The book mixes sound scripture interpretation with great illustrations of truth to personal application and action steps. You can tell I wholeheartedly recommend this book. I am now asking myself, 'How is your Luke 2:52?' Read this book!

– Rex Horne

President, Arkansas' Independent Colleges & Universities (former president of Ouachita Baptist University and former pastor of Immanuel Baptist Church of Little Rock)

Grow Like Jesus *has great insights about deepening our relationship with God and others. It gives very practical advice about how a person grows personally and spiritually. This study of the growth of Christ offers great perspectives and discernment that help all of us navigate to the full maturity that God has designed for us.*

– David A English

Leadership Development, Campus Crusade

Stephen Caldwell challenges the reader to Grow Like Jesus *through practical and straightforward steps that are relevant for new believers, as well as those more mature in their faith. His illustrations of 'real life' and attainable goals will encourage those who desire a deeper and more fulfilling walk with Christ to 'plant seeds' and 'yield fruit.' Luke 2:52 is one of my favorite passages and Stephen takes me back to my roots in exploring facets of Jesus' life that I should diligently care for and nourish. Not only will you buy this book for a friend, but you'll find yourself returning to its pages for wisdom and truth derived from the Scriptures.*

– **Mickey Rapier**
Directional Leader,
Fellowship Bible Church of Northwest Arkansas

If you are a brand new Christian, you have found the right book. If you have walked with Jesus for decades, you have found the right book. Whether you find yourself in the midst of running from God or you feel as close to God as you ever have, this book provides a way forward.

– **Nick Floyd**
Teaching Pastor, Cross Church, Fayetteville, Ark.

This book's focus on Jesus was well worth the review. While Scripture is filled to overflowing with godly guidelines for full life and growth on the Jesus journey, this simplification was quite refreshing. Who better than our Savior could be such a practical example?

– **Susan Addington**
Speaker, Mentor, Mother, and Author

One Christmas I asked my family who they felt would have the 'most challenging time' growing spiritually in the new year. They pointed at me with smiles – I think they were right. After many years of following Jesus, Grow Like Jesus *offers a simple way to find pockets of my inside world where I can continue to grow. That's very helpful.*

– Lloyd Reeb

Primary Spokesperson for Halftime and author of *From Success to Significance: when the pursuit of success is no longer enough*

Grow Like Jesus *is chock full of profound passages and principles. The practical and doable application steps will help you see real change, health, and balance in your life. Stephen writes from a rich history of walking with God and influencing others to also grow into the likeness of Jesus.*

– Steve Shadrach

Executive Director of Center for Mission Mobilization and author of *Brown Like Coffee, Viewpoints, The Fuel and the Flame,* and *The God Ask.*

Growing like Jesus either is or should be the primary goal of every follower of Christ. Our chief purpose in life and our chief desire, if we understand what He has done for us, is to bring God glory, and the way we do that is by learning more about Jesus in order to follow Him more closely. Grow Like Jesus *provides a deep dive into a Bible verse we often read right through. Although we don't know much about Jesus as a boy or young man, Stephen Caldwell shows there's plenty to be gleaned from Luke 2:52, anyway. There's more to learn about Jesus.*

– George Schroeder

National colleges writer, *USA TODAY*

I just finished reading Grow Like Jesus. *I found myself smiling right from the start because I felt such a connection to the personal stories. I really enjoyed the thought-provoking Pray, Read, Listen and Act passages. I also caught myself highlighting sections of the book along the way so I can circle back and ponder them some more. A lot of learning moments and definitely nourishment for the head and heart.*

– Denise McMahan

Founder/Publisher, CausePlanet.org

GROW

LIKE

JESUS

PRACTICING LUKE 2:52 DISCIPLESHIP

BY STEPHEN CALDWELL

Copyright © 2016

Editorial Work by Dave Troesh and AnnaMarie McHargue

Cover Design by Aaron Snethen

Interior Design by Aaron Snethen

Published in Boise, Idaho by Elevate Faith, a division of Elevate Publishing.

Web: www.elevatepub.com

For information please email info@elevatepub.com

ISBN (print): 9781943425204

Ebook ISBN: 9781943425570

Library Of Congress: 2015956304

Printed in the United States of America.

Scripture quotations marked NIV are taken from the Holy Bible, New International Version.® niv®. Copyright © 1973, 1978, 1984, by International Bible Society. Used by permission of Zondervan. All rights reserved.

DEDICATION

To my wife, Audrey, who, by the grace of God,
stepped into my life and became my joy.

Wow!

There's no greater proof that God
always provides us with something far better
than we could ever hope for or ask for!

The words printed here are concepts.
You must go through the experiences.

Saint Augustine

TABLE OF CONTENTS

FOREWORD

I want you to imagine that you are picking up the Bible for the first time. Perhaps no one told you where to begin, so you simply treat it as any other book, starting at the beginning and walking your way toward the end.

As you make your way through the Old Testament, you consistently see the Scriptures point to someone who is coming to bring salvation. You wonder who this man is. Finally, you arrive at the New Testament and everything becomes more clear.

You quickly read through the books of Matthew, Mark, Luke, and John. In incredible detail, these four Gospels lay out the life of Jesus. Yet as you reflect on these four records of the life of Jesus, your mind is drawn to something.

Part of the story is missing. It's as if there's a gap in the timeline. When you think about the thirty-three years that Jesus lived on this earth, you notice a very detailed account of his birth and a pretty clear picture of his ministry and death. But the years between his childhood and the start of his ministry at around age thirty are nowhere to be found in the canon of Scripture.

Instead, Luke gives us one statement that essentially sums up around two decades of Jesus' life – that He grew in wisdom, stature, and in favor with God and man (Luke 2:52). That's it. That's all we know.

So here's a question: Should this frustrate us or focus us?

I would portray to you that this gap in the story shouldn't push our hearts to frustration but should actually springboard us to a new and refreshed focus on our own spiritual growth before God.

We have everything we need. All that we need to know, we know. That's the confidence we can have any time we open up the pages of Scripture. What this really tells us about the Scriptures is that there is no end to its depths. The riches keep coming and coming. You can go deeper and deeper.

This book is a case in point. How does one write a book on one verse of the Bible? As highly as I think about this book and its author, Stephen Caldwell, I think this book speaks more to the depths of the riches of the Word of God than the depth of Stephen's thoughts. What Stephen has done in this book is to help you mine the wisdom of God in giving us this verse about the growing of Jesus and how that affects our own spiritual growth.

If you are a brand new Christian, you have found the right book. If you have walked with Jesus for decades, you have found the right book. Whether you find yourself in the midst of running from God or you feel as close to God as you ever have, this book provides a way forward. If you're ready to grow more like Jesus, continue reading.

- **Nick Floyd,** Teaching Pastor,
Cross Church, Fayetteville, Ark.

PREFACE

*"If you disapprove, I can only shrug
my shoulders. It's what I have."*

Stephen King

There are more than 31,000 verses in the Bible. This book is about one of them. That's it. One verse.

"One verse?" you say. "Can someone really write an entire book about one verse?"

Well, it's a short book, I'll admit. But it's also a powerful verse with plenty to say to those who are willing to listen.

So, yes, this is a book about just one verse. And that's plenty.

The verse — Luke 2:52 — spans the entire gap between Jesus the child and Jesus at the start of His ministry. I've tried to unpack the lessons of that verse in ways that are simple to understand but deep enough to drive meaningful changes in your life. And I've tried to equip you and challenge you to apply those lessons in your everyday life.

The more those lessons have emerged for me, the more I realized the value they can provide for all followers of Jesus. But they can be especially fruitful for anyone who is new to their faith in Christ or for anyone looking to breathe some new life into the dry bones of their existing faith.

I had known for some time that Luke 2:52 could have deep meaning for any follower of Jesus who was committed to growth. Now I was seeing an even bigger picture of how God might use it in the lives of His people. But I didn't start off with a God-sized goal. Years ago when I first came upon the verse and began to study its deeper meanings, I only really looked at how it applied to my kids and me.

At some point after giving my life to Jesus in the winter of 1991-92, I began looking for ways to more intentionally and proactively invest in the lives of my four children.

It's not that I wasn't involved in their lives already. I was. But I began to develop a deeper understanding of my role as a Godly father as opposed to my role as an any-old-run-of-the-mill father.

So in addition to helping with their homework, setting boundaries around their activities, and attending all of their sporting events and school programs, I wanted to connect with them in more personal ways. My hope was that we could learn from each other and develop a deeper trust that might last the rest of our lives.

This took on different forms for different children, because they all were at different ages and in different stages of life. But for my two younger children, this included weekly father-child breakfasts.

With my son, it wasn't always a hit. For one thing, Andrew was in junior high school. As you might imagine, he wasn't always a fan of getting up earlier than normal just so we could have enough time to go out for a sausage and biscuit. He was more of the roll-out-of-bed-as-late-as-possible type, much like his father at that age.

To make it worse, I wasn't very good at leading these meetings. And, frankly, they *felt* like meetings. I made them too formal. I thought they needed a structure, a plan. We needed to read a book together or work through some passage of the Bible or answer five questions or... well, we couldn't *just hang out and talk!*

I wanted to jump straight to a discipleship program, teach him to be a man! Plan the work and work the plan! Achieve results! Somewhere along the way, I forgot the real purpose — to deepen our relationships with God and each other.

Things improved with Lauren, my youngest daughter. She loved the idea of going to breakfast. It was an event. It was social. It was something different. It was, dare I say...fun. I wasn't sure if she liked spending time with me or if she just liked *going out*, and it really didn't matter to me. I liked spending time with her, and this was a great way to do it.

We quickly became regulars at Panera Bread Company on the north end of College Avenue in Fayetteville, Arkansas. We were on a first-name basis with the staff, and some of them literally watched Lauren grow up as we made our weekly bagel pilgrimage. I also learned to relax and keep things on a more relational level. We had structure at times, but mostly we just ate breakfast and talked about life.

During this same period, I had lunch one day with one of the pastors of Fellowship Bible Church of Northwest Arkansas, and we talked about this concept of "breakfast with dad." The pastor, Robert Cupp, had made a similar investment in his son's life, and he shared many of his wise ideas with me.

It was in those conversations that Robert mentioned Luke 2:52 — "And Jesus grew in wisdom and stature and in favor with God and man." — a simple but powerful verse that he had shared with his son and that I would share with my daughter. This little verse gave us structure without the formality. I could — and still can — simply ask my daughter, "So how's your Luke 2:52?" and she can share what's going on in the four areas of her life represented in that verse.

During those years when we were going to breakfast each week, I'd sometimes get a quick and vague answer: "It's all good." Other times we'd camp out on one area or another.

One year, as a Father's Day gift, Lauren painted me a hardboard plaque with Luke 2:52 written on it. It's one of my most treasured mementoes. It reminds me that "How's your Luke 2:52?" isn't a question that's just for adolescents — it's for me, too. It's for all of us.

Too often, Luke 2:52 is seen as a verse for kids growing up, but it's more than that. It's a verse that can help shape our walk with Christ from the moment we yield to His authority until the moment He brings us into His presence in heaven.

Simply put, the verse is a model for growing like Jesus.

Faith in Christ is a one-time decision that leads to a lifetime of growth. If we want to grow in our faith in God and in our relationship with God, then what better model than to *Grow Like Jesus*?

The verse itself, of course, is simple. You can sum it up in a few straightforward sentences, put it on a Post-it Note, and hold yourself accountable to it daily. My vision for this book is that it helps you aspire to something more, just as it has helped me. I believe it can help you develop a deeper understanding of what it means to grow in wisdom, in stature, and in favor with God and man. And I believe it can start you on the path of discovery, or rediscovery, of life-changing growth in those areas.

Whether you're just now awakening to a life with this fellow named Jesus or you've been friends with Him for decades, you can live out this verse daily and more fully *Grow Like Jesus*.

Section I

PLANTING SEEDS

CHAPTER 1
FIGURE IT OUT

"It's so much easier to suggest solutions when you don't knowtoo much about the problem."

Malcolm S. Forbes

I was on a family vacation once on the southern end of the Outer Banks of North Carolina when several of us decided to go on a short sailing adventure.

We chartered a boat with a captain who would take us across the sound from Atlantic Beach to Beaufort, a town on the inland coast. Half of our group would drive to Beaufort and the other half would sail there; then we would swap up — those who drove would sail back and those who sailed over would drive back.

We left the dock and our captain — Captain Peggy — began issuing orders. As we prepared to hoist the sails, she instructed one of my brothers-in-law to turn the helm to the right and hold it. He did, but apparently he turned it too hard and for too long. The cable from the helm to the rudder snapped, and we became the proverbial ship without a rudder.

As we floundered in the middle of the shipping lane, Captain Peggy radioed her boss to report the problem. A few minutes later, we watched as another sailboat left the dock and headed our way. We then watched as it kept right on going, taking another group of tourists on a sailing adventure and leaving us to rock in its wake.

Captain Peggy got back on the radio, and her boss was more direct and clear this time about what would happen. To paraphrase, he said, "Figure it out."

And Captain Peggy did just that. She figured it out. She applied a formula I've seen in leadership books from time to time — necessity + creativity + persistence = resourcefulness. She figured out a way to somehow manually work the rudder and steer us on our journey.

That's life, right? Figure it out. You may have instructions, or you may not. And even if you have instructions, sometimes they are lacking what you really need for the circumstances you face. To keep moving, you simply have to figure it out.

Whether we're in a difficult predicament — floundering in the shipping lanes of life — or just trying to learn how to live better in the day-to-day realities we face, that's what we're doing. We're just trying to figure it out.

When doing that, I typically find myself starting with the same key question: *What's that look like?* Stephen Covey, author of 7 *Habits of Highly Effective People*, called it "Begin with the End in Mind" (It's habit Number Two). If we can picture what success looks like, we can work out the details of how to achieve it.

It doesn't matter what I'm learning — how to dance the West Coast Swing, how to replace a carburetor on a truck, how to use a new math formula, or how to fix the rudder on a sailboat in the middle of the bay — it helps to visualize the result and the process.

We might not always voice the question, but most of us at least think it.

What's that look like?

For generations, writers have heard the instructor's wisdom along the same lines when it comes to story-telling: *Show me, don't tell me.* It's good advice. People want to visualize. They want to see it, personalize it, understand how it works in real life, not just as words on paper. They want to see *what it looks like* so they can relate to it and figure it out.

And let's face it: We typically want the picture painted in as much detail as possible. We want the writer or instructor to give us specific details, a step-by-step process for moving along so we can complete our project or vision. The last thing we want is for the writer or instructor to radio from the shore with this message: "Figure it out." We want him to come fix it or at least send us comprehensive instructions for how to fix it ourselves. Pictures and a YouTube video would be nice.

If you're like me, when it comes to life, you're regularly trying to "figure it out." Thankfully, God filled the Bible with examples and illustrations that show us in detail what it looks like to live according to His will. Then again, He also filled the Good Book with the exact opposite — passages that tell us in broad strokes what to do but leave it up to us to figure out the details.

For instance, Matthew 28:16-20, the passage known as the Great Commission, tells us to "go and make disciples of all nations," but it doesn't tell us how to do it. You see it modeled in the lives of people like the Apostle Paul, but not once does it say that you have to meet someone for breakfast once a week and work through a Max Lucado or Joyce Meyer book.

Even when Jesus uses parables to illustrate the things He's teaching, He often leaves open the "what's that look like for me?" question for us to answer when it comes to our own lives.

Figure it out.

This, I believe, is one way God draws us closer to Him. Sometimes He tells us what to do and how to do it, and sometimes He allows us to figure it out on our own. In that process, we have the option and opportunity of giving ourselves to God and growing closer to Him. We can seek to know Him and please Him and bring Him glory, and in doing so we can experience an intimacy that otherwise is lost to us.

My beautiful wife points out that this holds true in human relationships, as well. You know, like my relationship with her. I prefer it when she tells me what she wants. I ask questions like, "How can I serve you? How can I please you? How can I love you better?" If she'll just tell me what she wants, I'll do it. And, at times, that works rather well. She tells me what she wants or needs, and I do my best to give it to her. She's thankful, and I feel good.

But when I figure out her needs and satisfy them on my own without asking or her explaining, we draw even closer. There's a deeper intimacy, because I've taken the time and made the effort to understand her and know her well enough to anticipate her needs and provide for them. I've made the effort not just to *serve* her, but also to *know* her.

In the same way, God sometimes gives us very clear direction and other times He allows us the privilege of discovering Him and trusting in Him so that we can bring Him glory even when He isn't hitting us over the head with a commandment.

When we get creative in figuring out a way to "make disciples," for instance, we're tapping into something unique in us that God created. And we're trusting that

He will provide direction and answers in ways so mysterious that we can't take credit for figuring it out — we figured it out, but we give God the credit. I believe that brings Him glory and pleasure, while developing intimacy between the Creator and His creation.

This book offers an opportunity for you to explore one of those special passages in Scripture that seems rather broad but that can lead to intimacy with God as you trust Him to help you figure out "what that looks like" in your daily life.

Luke 2:52 provides guidelines you can follow, and I have offered some direction on where you can take it. There are only a few chapters, and they aren't particularly long. The final five chapters all include questions and suggestions for things you can do that might help you figure out how you can grow like Jesus. You can work through those on your own, in a one-on-one discipleship relationship, or with your small group. You don't have to figure it out alone.

Maybe you see Luke 2:52 as simple and obvious. "I got it, God," you say. "What's next?" But the deeper you go into this powerful verse and apply it to your life, the better you can understand God, the more you can anticipate what He asks of you and what He created you for, the greater your intimacy with the Lord of the universe, and the more you can *Grow Like Jesus.*

CHAPTER 2
GROOM

*If we do not plant knowledge when young,
it will give us no shade when we are old.*

Lord Chesterfield

Have you ever wondered about the life of Jesus — the parts that aren't told in the historical record?

You know: What was He like in those run-of-the-mill family moments as a child? Was it even possible for Jesus to have an "ordinary" moment? What games did He play with friends? What types of things did He build asa young carpenter? Did He ever have a "heart-to-heart" talk with His earthly father? Did He snore? Sneeze? Give people "funny looks?" Did He chase fireflies at night? Did He ever think out loud in stream-of-consciousness fashion, or was every word carefully measured? Did He skip rocks across the water while envisioning the day when He would walk on it? How well could He sing or draw? Did His voice "change" as teenager? What was His favorite color? Did He perform miracles when no one was looking?

When we consider the life of Jesus, most of us focus on the alpha and the omega — the beginning and the end. We start with the miraculous entry of God into human form and then move quickly to His three-year ministry, death on the cross, and, of course, the resurrection.

Womb, boom, tomb, and bloom!

There's more, of course. There always is with Jesus. As the author and perfector of our faith, one-third of the Trinity, the only human to possess divinity, the One who whispered the universe into existence with what some think of as a big bang, Jesus can't be fully defined, much less defined in simple terms. His layers aren't just multiple, they are extra-dimensional — existing outside of time and space and into dimensions we don't even know about as mere human beings.

And, yet, he lived on Earth as a baby, as a boy, as a teenager, as a young man.

What was He like, this baby, this boy, this teenager, this young man who was God?

You could argue, of course, that the things recorded about the life of Jesus are plenty fascinating. And, in fact, you could argue that we know exactly what we need to know — no more and no less. If we needed more, God would have inspired more of the authors who told His story in the old and new testaments. If we needed less, God would have given those authors more memory lapses. We know what we know, and it's more than we can comprehend as it is. Who can fully understand Jesus? He's God. So why waste time asking questions about what's not described in the Bible?

Because our purpose on this planet, as the saying goes, is to "know God and make Him known."

The writer of Chronicles put it this way: "Give praise to the LORD, proclaim His name; make known among the nations what He has done." *(1 Chronicles 16:8)*

Jesus drove the point home when describing His mission on Earth: "Righteous Father, though the world does not know you, I know you, and they know that you have sent Me. I have made You known to them, and will continue to make You known in order that the love You have for Me may be in them and that I myself may be in them." *(John 17:25-26)*

Anything we can learn about the Lord of lords and King of kings is a good thing for us and a glorifying thing for God. So we read the Scriptures with fresh eyes, a fresh heart, and ever-changing circumstances, and while the words never change and the truth never changes, our insights into those words and their truth can unfold in unimaginable ways.

But unless we read and believe the Apocryphal writings, we don't know much about Jesus between the ages of about 12 to 33.

Or do we?

***

Alpha and Omega. Beginning and End. The story of Jesus, of course, begins in pre-time, before the formation of the universe that He spoke into existence. He is part of the story from the beginning. He shows up throughout the Old Testament as prophet after prophet foretells His coming and gives insights into His nature, His purpose, and His character.

Jesus in theory; real but still abstract.

Then humanity meets Him in an exciting new way — in person, face to face. The prophecies literally take on life. God becomes human, takes on flesh and blood, and the story of mankind takes a dramatic shift.

You know the big-picture details.

A young virgin finds herself pregnant and gives birth to the Son of God.

When the time is right, He enters into the ministry as an itinerant rabbi.

His cousin baptizes Him, and then He spends about three years preaching about the Kingdom of God.

His message and methods tick off the powers that be, so they conspire to rid the world of Him. They claim victory when they see Jesus nailed to a cross and then buried in a grave that's sealed with a big rock. He's dead. Game over. Life can go back to normal.

But, of course, Jesus flips normal on its head in a huge way. He defeats death. In doing so, He bridges the gap for all humanity to access God.

None of us are worthy of spending eternity with God, regardless of how well we live our lives or think we've lived our lives. Jesus, the One who was/is good enough, took on our sins with His death; He literally died and went to hell and back to save us.

That's the "womb, boom, tomb, and bloom" story — unimaginable birth, dynamic ministry, tragic death, and impossible resurrection.

So what's missing from that story that we might look into more deeply?

Groom.

How did Jesus go from a boy to a man? How did He prepare for the most significant ministry in the history of the world? How was He groomed for manhood? For His role as rabbi? For His destiny as Savior of the world?

That's the story of Luke 2:52.

***

There are plenty of written accounts of Jesus the boy, but most of them aren't canonized — recognized as authentic, God-inspired Scripture.

So here's what we know from the Gospels...

Matthew tells us that Jesus and His family moved to Egypt shortly after His birth to avoid the wrath of Herod the Great.

After His birth, but not immediately after it as the common Christmas telling would indicate, Jesus was worshipped by the Magi. These "wise men" were warned in a dream that Herod feared this child as a threat to his rule, so they didn't tell the king where he could find the King. When he realized the Magi had skipped town without giving up the child's whereabouts, Herod ordered the death of all first-born sons under the age of two who lived in or near Bethlehem. Joseph and Mary had been warned by the Holy Spirit. That's what took them to Egypt.

At some point after Herod died, which historians estimate was two to four years after the birth of Jesus, the family moved back to Israel and settled in Nazareth. Matthew points these facts out to show how the prophecies had been fulfilled. Then he moves on to the baptism of Jesus as an adult ready to begin His ministry.

Mark starts with the baptism of Jesus by His cousin John, skipping the birth and pre-ministry years altogether.

In the Gospel of John, the story of Jesus begins pre-time.

"In the beginning was the Word, and the Word was with God, and the Word was God. He was with God in the beginning. Through Him all things were made; without Him nothing was made that has been made. In Him was life, and that life was the light of all mankind. The light shines in the darkness, and the darkness has not overcome it." *(John 1:1-5)*

His opening points are that God had become man — that the Light of the World had actually entered the world. *(v. 9)* Then he, too, moves on to the baptism by John and the actual ministry of Jesus.

Luke provides a more historical narrative and provides the most information about the early years of Jesus. After his detailed account of the birth story, Luke spends about 30 verses on Jesus the boy.

Jesus was eight days old when, in keeping with Jewish tradition, He was circumcised and officially given His name. When He was still an infant, Joseph and Mary took Him to Jerusalem for a ritual ceremony at the temple. Mary, by Jewish law, had to wait about 40 days for "cleansing" after giving birth, and then the family could take the child to the temple to present Him and offer a sacrifice to God.

This is when he encounters Simeon and then Anna.

Simeon, who is described as "righteous and devout," *(Luke 2:25)* had been promised by the Holy Spirit that he would live to see the Messiah. When he saw Jesus as a baby, he immediately proclaimed that the promise had been fulfilled in the child.

Anna, an elderly widow who lived in the temple and is described as a prophet, saw the encounter with Simeon and affirmed that Jesus was the Messiah. "Coming up to them at that very moment, she gave thanks to God and spoke about the child to all who were looking forward to the redemption of Jerusalem." *(Luke 2:38)*

Luke skips the migration to Egypt and picks things back up when Jesus is 12 years old living in Nazareth. This is one of those stories that parents find intriguing, because it's hard not to read it without putting yourself in their place.

They had gone to Jerusalem for the Festival of the Passover and, while on their way home, they lost their child.

That's right: They lost Jesus.

They lost the One who had come to seek and save the lost.

It's frightening enough to lose your child in a mall or department store or to have a child wander away for a few minutes in the park, but Joseph and Mary had traveled a full day before realizing Jesus wasn't tagging along.

These clearly weren't helicopter parents, hovering over their child's every move like we so often see in modern America. But don't bash them too quickly for what might look like negligence or indifference. They were living in a different time and place, a time and place when children stayed with the extended group and the extended group watched the children.

When they went back to Jerusalem, they looked for three days (I wonder where they looked?) before they found Jesus at the temple courts hanging out with the rabbis, "listening to them and asking them questions" *(v. 46)* — and apparently doing some teaching Himself.

The other teachers were "amazed at His understanding and His answers," *(v. 47)* but His mom, while "astonished," also was a bit ticked off. She said the equivalent of "What were You doing?! You worried me to death!"

This seemed to catch Jesus by surprise, if that's possible.

"Why were you searching for Me?" He asked. "Didn't you know I had to be in My Father's house?" *(v. 49)*

As if to make it clear that Jesus was, indeed, a "good boy," Luke points out that His parents didn't understand His response and that they all went back to Nazareth, where Jesus was "obedient to them."

Luke tells us that Mary "treasured all these things in her heart," *(v. 51)* and then ends Chapter 2 with his summary of the rest of Jesus' youth and young adulthood — "And Jesus grew in wisdom and stature, and in favor with God and man." *(Luke 2:52)*

So we don't know if Jesus really performed miracles while living in Egypt or if He caught fireflies at night or if He went to sleepovers with His friends. But we know He wasn't just hanging around eating lentils and pomegranates.

We know He was growing in four specific areas: Wisdom, stature, favor with God, and favor with people.

First, He was growing, and not just physically. Growth involves change from one state to another, from root to fruit, from a child to a man. The Greek word used here means to "progress, advance" and, in the original sense, "to make one's way forward by chopping away obstacles."

Growth isn't easy, and it requires effort. Jesus was God, but He also was a human. He developed. He matured. He aged. He chopped away obstacles so He could advance. He grew.

Second, He grew in specific areas.

He grew in wisdom, which means He learned things. This is a mystery that we'll examine in more detail later, but the point for now is that He grew His intellect and understanding.

He also grew in stature, which means He got taller and that He took care of His body. He matured physically. (Luke 2:40 notes that Jesus grew "stronger" as He grew in stature.)

Finally, He grew in favor with God and man, which means He grew His critical relationships. He developed His relationships with His Father and with other people.

Wisdom, stature, favor with God, favor with man.

Intellectual, physical, spiritual, social.

As it turns out, and it shouldn't be a surprise, growth in these four areas continues to prepare us for success in life — the type of the success that can come with hardships but that allows us to know God and make Him known. In other words, *real success.*

Section II
YIELDING FRUIT

CHAPTER 3
WISDOM

*"What good is knowledge without fear of God?...
A humble rustic who serves God is better than a
proud intellectual who neglects his soul to study
the course of the stars."*

Thomas à Kempis

Picture the ladies of Nazareth, circa 17 A.D.

It's shortly after noon, and the sun is warm. They're standing on the dust-covered courtyard, talking among themselves as they go about their daily chores.

"That Jesus," one of them says, "He's sure a sharp one."

"Oh, yes, and such a good boy," says another. "Smart and good to His mother."

"Mary should be so proud," the third one says. "He'll make a fine rabbi."

"Oh, yes, a fine rabbi, that Jesus," another concurs. "So smart. So smart. And good to His mother."

Jesus was a smart man.

Now there's a shocker. But how smart? And how'd he get so smart? Was he born all-knowing — an omni-genius from birth?

Great question. Ask three theologians and you'll get two dozen answers. Or, better yet, we can ask Jesus together when we all get to heaven.

In the meantime, let's fall back on the fact that Luke 2:52 tells us Jesus *grew in wisdom*. This would indicate His first words weren't a recitation of the Pythagorean theorem, and He wasn't engaging in Epistemological debates while putting together blocks with other toddlers.

It's impossible to say for sure how the supernatural Jesus meshed with the human Jesus when it came to His intelligence. As God, Jesus knows everything, remembers everything, and understands everything. Yet, there were times when He didn't seem to tap into that reservoir — when, as theologians say, "He laid aside His prerogative."

What a mystery!

And as a person, Jesus could relate to our struggles. He felt things, including temptations. And He grew, and not just physically. So if Jesus needed to grow His wisdom while He walked about the earth, then the rest of us need to do so as well.

What's that look like? In other words, what is wisdom and how do we grow it?

Let's start by examining what it is.

***

Christopher Michael Langan grew up in poverty, but he was reading by the age of three. He reportedly fell asleep while taking the SAT, but still managed a perfect score on the test. His IQ is supposedly between 195 and 210.

His occupation? Rancher.

Langan dropped out of college but continued to study on his own. He's known for his intellectual writings and theories, but his income has come from working mainly in manual labor jobs — construction worker, cowboy, bouncer, etc.

Is he the smartest person in America, as some claim?

William James Sidis entered Harvard University when he was 11 years old, two years after he was accepted into the Ivy League college and nine years after he began reading the *New York Times* on his own.

He eventually learned to speak more than 40 languages, and his IQ reportedly was 275 — one of the highest ever recorded. But he spent much of his adult life doing menial tasks and writing under pseudonyms to avoid the limelight.

Was he the smartest person ever, as some claim?

Langan and Sidis exemplify a natural intelligence that most of us would say can't be taught or learned or grown. Some folks are just smarter than others, right?

That, of course, doesn't make them wise or even successful. Many of the smartest people on the planet struggle with relationships. They have low EI — Emotional Intelligence — so they don't play (or work) well with others. And research now indicates that determination — or grit, as some researchers call it — is a better predictor of success than smarts.

Solomon remains the person many of us identify as the wisest to ever live, because the Bible describes him in just that way. Solomon asked God for wisdom and knowledge, and God, as is His pattern, delivered way more than anyone could have imagined. 1 Kings and 2 Chronicles go on and on about the wisdom of Solomon.

What did Solomon's wisdom look like? We know that Solomon spoke "three thousand proverbs" and more than a "thousand" songs. We know he understood plant life, animals — birds, reptiles, and fish — and that "all the kings of the world" sent people to listen to Solomon when they heard of his wisdom. The Queen of Sheba was so impressed by Solomon's wisdom that she was "overwhelmed" by it and ended up praising God for it.

To sum it up, Solomon's wisdom was artistic, intellectual, relational, and, most of all, it brought glory to God.

When Jesus grew His wisdom He wasn't necessarily growing His intelligence. Then again, just because wisdom isn't *all* about intelligence doesn't mean that it has *nothing* to do with intelligence. In fact, there is a strong connection between wisdom and intelligence, at least as it is used in Luke 2:52.

The Greek word *sophia,* the root of English terms like *sophisticated* and *philosophy*, translates as "wisdom, insight, skill, (human or divine) intelligence," according to Strong's Concordance. This is the word Luke uses twice in Chapter 2 to describe the Son of God.

Thayer's Greek Lexicon spends a good bit of space defining the word, but starts this way: "The wisdom which belongs to men: universally, Luke 2:40, 52; specifically, the varied knowledge of things human and divine, acquired by acuteness and experience, and summed up in maxims and proverbs..."

So wisdom, as used in Luke 2:52, includes the combination of insight, skill, and intelligence that we can grow to better understand our world and the God who created us.

We know Jesus was book smart. He knew the Torah. Jesus listened and learned. As noted earlier, Luke points out that as a 12-year-old Jesus was paying attention to the rabbis and asking them questions — and apparently pushing them to think differently with His insightful words.

Wisdom, for Jesus, included knowledge of "things human and divine," but it wasn't just book smarts. His wisdom also included those things "acquired by acuteness and experience."

In other words, He was insightful. He understood what was happening around Him and how everything fit together — the facts, the history, the people, and the relationships. Jesus had a high IQ and a high EI, not to mention the ability to meld it all together through common sense. And He had immeasurable determination — a focus on doing His Father's will, even when it meant dying a horrific death nailed to a cross.

Jesus also understood the connection between His thought life and wisdom — the reality that our thoughts shapeour attitudes, words, and actions. As James Allen put it in his classic, *As A Man Thinketh*, "Act is the blossom of thought, and joy and suffering are its fruits; thus does a man garner in the sweet and bitter fruitage of his own husbandry."

The more disciplined we are in our thoughts, the greater wisdom we'll display in our words and actions, and the more we'll experience joy over suffering.

If we focus our thoughts on sinful temptations, we'll find ourselves drawn into the snares of pride, arrogance, envy, lust, gossip, greed...If we focus our thoughts on the things of God, we'll find ourselves living in humility and trusting in God for our every need — including our next thought. If we're in tune to God's Word and to the Holy Spirit, the words and actions that come out of us are more likely to reflect God's holiness than our sinfulness.

Proverbs 28:26 says, "Those who trust in themselves are fools, but those who walk in wisdom are kept safe." Author Sarah Young puts a nice spin on that verse in *Jesus Calling*, saying, "The essence of wisdom is to trust in (God) more than in yourself or other people." And Paul put it this way: "The mind governed by the flesh is death, but the mind governed by the Spirit is life and peace." *(Romans 8:6)*

James describes the wisdom that "comes from heaven" as first of all "pure" and then as "peace-loving, considerate, submissive, full of mercy and good fruit, impartial and sincere." *(James 3:17)* And he says that humility "comes from wisdom." *(James 3:13)*

James also talks about a different kind of wisdom — the kind that is "earthly, unspiritual, demonic." That wisdom leads to "bitter envy and selfish ambition." *(James 3:14-15)*

In a small group Bible study my wife and I were leading, there's a commentary on James 3:9-18 that describes wisdom as, "a deep-seated understanding [that] comes from God, enabling us to live and speak according to His Word."

That's a lot of wise teaching on the meaning of wisdom. I don't know about you, but I need something more concise that I can get my limited mind around. So, here is how I define the wisdom that Jesus grew: "Knowledge and insight from God that benefits you and others and brings glory to God."

If the knowledge and insights don't come from God, they aren't wise. If they don't bring glory to God, they aren't wise. If they come from God, they will benefit everyone and they will bring glory to God. That's wisdom.

***

Sound like something all of us could use? Of course.

There is value in wisdom, and the Scriptures speak of it frequently and with variety. The first seven chapters of Proverbs, in fact, make point after point about the value of wisdom, as well as where it comes from, what it looks like, and how to attain it.

Listen to this poetic description from Proverbs 3:13-18:

Blessed are those who find wisdom,

those who gain understanding,

for she is more profitable than silver

and yields better returns than gold.

She is more precious than rubies;

nothing you desire can compare with her.

Long life is in her right hand;

in her left hand are riches and honor.

Her ways are pleasant ways,

and all her paths are peace.

She is a tree of life to those who take hold of her;

those who hold her fast will be blessed.

Throughout the "wisdom" books—Proverbs, Psalms, Song of Solomon, Job, Ecclesiastes, and James — we find time and time again different ways that God tells us what wisdom is, new examples of what it looks like, and practical advice on how to get it.

So how do we get this wisdom that's so important to our lives? We can't buy wisdom at the local department store. Our parents can't give it to us, although they can pass along some good genes and some great advice. Our friends, teachers, mentors, and bosses can't give it to us, although they can help us grow it.

Ultimately, it still falls on us — as individuals — to seek it, to go get it, and that's not always easy. Wisdom is elusive because our sin nature rejects it, and Satan, the king of lies, distorts it.

Job, regarded as the oldest book in the Bible, addresses it, well, wisely. "But where is wisdom found?" he asks. "No human knows the way. Nor can it be discovered in the deepest sea...Where then is wisdom? It is hidden from human eyes and even from birds. Death and destruction have merely heard rumors about where it is found." *(Job 28:12-14; 20-22, CEV)*

Then comes the kicker:

"God is the only one who knows the way to wisdom, because He sees everything beneath the heavens. When God divided out the wind and the water, and when He decided the path for rain and lightning, He also determined the truth and defined wisdom. God told us, 'Wisdom means that you respect Me, the Lord, and turn from sin.'" *(Job 28:23-28, CEV)*

Quick quiz: What's the wisest decision you can ever make?

Answer: Respect the Lord and turn from your sin.

That's salvation — eternal salvation. That's a wise choice.

That type of wisdom, like all real wisdom, comes, as Job points out, from God. So to attain and grow wisdom in our daily lives, we turn first to God in awe and respect.

Proverbs 2:6 says, "For the Lord gives wisdom; from His mouth come knowledge and understanding."

But as Job points out, God isn't a cosmic vending machine that dispenses wisdom to anyone who asks. Instead, our pursuit of wisdom begins with our relationship with God.

We respect God for who he is — God, big G. The Psalmist tells us that the "fear of the Lord is the beginning of wisdom." *(Psalm 111:10; also see Proverbs 1:7 and 9:10)* This is where so many intellectuals get off track and are left with knowledge that lacks wisdom. When believe our knowledge is the source of our wisdom rather than God, arrogance takes over. Thomas à Kempis said, "What good is knowledge without fear of God?...A humble rustic who serves God is better than a proud intellectual who neglects his soul to study the course of the stars."

Humility isn't just a responsibility as we grow in wisdom; it's an inevitability. Fearing God humbles us and prepares us for God's wisdom. That wisdom humbles us all the more. And when we fear God, that respect drives us to respond wisely. And the wisest decision we can make? Back to Job 28:23-28: We turn from sin.

The older and newer testaments both speak of wisdom as a gift from the Holy Spirit.

In Exodus 35, Moses tells us about two men who helped build the tabernacle, Bezalel and Oholiab. He says God filled Bezalel with "the Spirit of God, with wisdom, with understanding, with knowledge, and with all kinds of skills — to make artistic designs for work in gold, silver, and bronze, to cut and set stones, to work in wood and to engage in all kinds of artistic crafts." *(Exodus 35:31-33)*

Joshua was "filled with the spirit of wisdom" *(Deuteronomy 34:9)* and Daniel was described (by the queen of Babylon) as a man who has "the spirit of the holy gods in him" and who had "insight and intelligence and wisdom like that of the gods." *(Daniel 5:11)*

Paul talks about wisdom and knowledge as gifts from the Spirit. *(Ephesians 1:17, I Corinthians 12:7-8)*

And James tells us, "If any of you lacks wisdom, you should ask God, who gives generously to all without finding fault, and it will be given to you." *(James 1:5)*

If we've opened our hearts to the Lord and put Him in the proper place in our lives, then we've opened ourselves up to one of His greatest gifts — wisdom. This is the intersection in our daily lives where He speaks to us through His word and through the Holy Spirit, and we respond in obedience with our natural, God-given gifts and skills.

A circular process develops. We fear God and give our lives to Him. As a result, we put our trust in God and develop a desire to know Him more deeply and more intimately. This causes us to read more, study more, spend more time in prayer, which, of course, grows our overall intelligence and our understanding of who God really is, how we should relate to Him, and how He wants us to relate to other people. And the more we learn about God, the more compelled we are to fear His name and respect His authority over our lives. This drives more humility within us and a greater dependence on God, which brings us back to an increased desire to know even more about Him and how we can bring glory to His name.

As the cycle continues, wisdom grows.

Go Forth and Grow It

It's common to think wisdom is something we display — that it's about providing our sage advice to the people around us. Personally, I struggle with confidence in believing that my advice is worth sharing. I don't think of myself as all that wise.

But that's not the point.

We should pray for wisdom and for opportunities to share wisdom with others. That's how we share the gospel, disciple, mentor, and counsel. But wisdom, first and foremost, is about our relationship with God. To grow in wisdom, we grow in that relationship. If we do that, the fruit of sharing it with others will follow and we will wisely trust God for the words to say and for any results that might come from them.

Questions

- How would you personally define wisdom?

- Who are the three wisest people you know and interact with regularly? What are a few of their attributes that caused you to think of them as "wise?"

- The Queen of Sheba praised God for Solomon's wisdom. Who is influenced by the wisdom you grow?

- How have you seen the discipline (or lack of discipline) in your thought life connect to your actions?

- How do others respond to you when you display wisdom? How do they respond to God?

- How is that last answer different depending on how you define "others" – your spouse, your children, your friends, your co-workers, the clerk at a store, a homeless person who asks for a handout, etc.?

- List the attributes of God you fear. List the attributes you respect. What is your response to these attributes?

- Read and think through the "wisdom cycle" at the end of the chapter. How are you taking intentional steps in that process? Are you seeing evidence of personal growth in the area of wisdom?

Go-Do's

Consider these sources for growing wisdom and come up with ways you can tap into them more regularly:

Pray: Boldly pray to God about wisdom. Ask the Holy Spirit to fill you with wisdom. Ask God to help you slow down and listen to Him. Praise Him for every insight that comes your way. Prayer isn't just something we do at mealtime or bedtime. It's a state of heart and mind. The Bible tells us to "pray without ceasing." (*1 Thessalonians 5:16-18*) It's something we can do as we begin and end the day, but also as we begin a work task and as we seek God's insights in our lives. For instance, pray before you listen to a sermon or before you read the Scriptures or before you have lunch with a friend. Ask God to open your mind and heart to what he wants from you and for you.

Read: Start with the Word of God. Read the Bible every day, but don't just read it, ponder it. Allow it to soak into your very soul. Carve out a specific time for daily reading of Scripture. My wife and I read a devotional and pray together each morning, then read Scripture and pray before we go to bed. We begin and end our day with God. In between, we both do our best to defeat the distractions of the world by seeking God in the moment. It's not easy, and, in fact, we often come up short. But the more we find ourselves doing this, the more peace we find, regardless of the circumstances of our life. Supplement God's word — but never replace it — with devotionals, articles, and books by Bible-believing authors. See Appendix 1 for some recommended readings.

Listen: The art of listening might be lost on most people in the modern world, but it's lost none of its value. Listening, of course, is a vital part of prayer. We don't just talk to God in prayer, we listen. "Be still and know that I am God," he tells us. *(Psalm 46:10)* We also need to drive out arrogance and pride in our lives by listening to other Godly men and women. Regularly attend a good church and listen to the Godly, Bible-based preaching and teaching. Take part in Bible studies. Form an accountability group with trusted and trustworthy men or women (men if you're a man, women if you're a woman); share openly and transparently with this group and listen to what they tell you.

Act: As you pray, read, and listen, God no doubt will speak to you in some amazing ways. He will encourage you and He will enlighten you as you grow closer to Him and, thus, wiser. But He will also challenge you. He will speak to you in ways that ask you to leave your comfort zone. He might not speak to you, however, with specific instructions. So you must learn to act in obedience when you're confident in what He's saying and act in faith when you're unsure. Trust Him above all else, go wherever He directs you to go, and do whatever He directs you to do. That's wisdom, and it leads to more wisdom. Oswald Chambers, in his typically blunt fashion said, "God's revelations are sealed to us until they are opened to us by obedience. God will never reveal more truth about Himself 'til you obey what you know already."

CHAPTER 4
STATURE

"A bear, however hard he tries, grows tubby without exercise."

Winnie-the-Pooh (A.A. Milne)

My wife and I strive to eat a healthy diet. By healthy, I mean we generally eat foods that are good for us, and, for the most part, we avoid foods that put our health at risk.

Millions of people around the world share that commitment, and, yet, few (if any) approach it in exactly the same way we do— or in the same way as anyone else.

For instance, when I said that we eat foods that are "good for us," certain things probably popped in your mind — maybe that we're vegetarians or vegan.

For you, a "healthy diet" might mean you get a Diet Coke with your super value meal. For someone else, it's no carbs. For another, it's all carbs.

And what puts your health at risk? Alcohol? Cigarettes? Donuts? Red meat? All meat? Bread? Dairy?

Experts the world over have opinions on what we should and shouldn't eat, not to mention how and how much we should exercise. These experts write articles and books sharing the findings of their research, and they express — with great confidence — their beliefs on the topic of physical health and, if you want the term *de-jure*, "wellness."

You can find plenty of authors, for instance, promoting a "Biblical" diet. What did Moses eat? What did Noah eat? What did Jesus eat?

Audrey and I once went to a presentation on the popular "Paleo Diet." Proponents believe humans are genetically adapted to the environment of the Paleolithic time period. They say our bodies haven't adapted to properly digest newer foods, including grains, legumes, and dairy. So we should only eat foods that mimic foods from the Paleo era.

The Paleo era was way back in the way-back days when pre-historic folks were just figuring out how to make tools out of stones. Depending upon your view of the age of our planet, that era was either around 2.6 million years ago or between 6,000 and 10,000 years ago. Either way, it wouldn't have included any of the modern processed foods.

With this approach, in other words, you eat what the cavemen ate (and the cavewomen and cavechildren). And just what did they eat? Not much, apparently. And even less of the stuff I love. No bread, for instance. No milk, either.

My response at the time, which, by the way, wasn't endorsed by my wife: "Jesus ate bread."

And he drank wine.

But, as my wife is quick to point out, the food and drink of His day isn't nearly the same as the food and drink of our day. In time, I've come to agree with her. (Strange how many husbands eventually come around to their wife's ways of thinking.)

She and I now generally follow the healthy lifestyle approach of *The Daniel Plan*, a book by pastor Rick Warren and physicians Daniel Amen and Mark Hyman. It's a holistic approach that involves faith, food, fitness, focus, and friends. (I think it's fabulous, not to mention fantastic and fascinating, by the way, that all the things you need to stay healthy begin with the same letter!)

I've learned to eat and enjoy real food — stuff that's not processed in a plant but that actually grows as a plant, and meat that was grass-fed and not force-fed, injected, or raised in cages.

Our bodies have been over-conditioned to crave what's bad for us, but Audrey and I have discovered the benefits of real, whole foods that taste great and keep us mentally, physically, and spiritually sharper.

This change in diet was a big shift for me — I used to consider myself a meat-and-potatoes-aterian. My two favorite meals growing up were pot roast and pizza (loaded with meats and cheeses, of course). I still love pot roast and pizza, but people can change. Not too long ago I took a photo of my plate and sent it to my mother, a nutritionist by profession, who fought the seemingly fruitless battles during my youth to get me to eat anything green. Our dinner that night: Roasted yellow cauliflower with roasted tomatoes and salmon.

Who is this strange person I have become? I wondered while looking at that plate. *Someone much better off*, I concluded.

***

So what's all that have to do with how Jesus grew?

Well, now we're getting back into that great big realm of the unknown.

Luke 2:52 tells us only that Jesus grew in stature.

The English word *stature* has two meanings. One involves the physical and has synonyms like "build, height, physique, figure, tallness, and size." The other is about relevance within a group: standing, importance, prominence, status, rank, and reputation. Luke 2:52 speaks to that type of relevance when it says Jesus grew "in favor with...man."

The word stature, as it's used in this verse, means height, full age, and time of life. So when it says Jesus grew "in stature," it's talking about the physical maturation of Jesus.

In this case, in other words, it simply means that He grew up physically. He got taller. He grew into adulthood.

If you want to get picky — and we should get picky when we interpret Scripture — I think that's all the verse tells us. Even in its most simple, straightforward form, however, the description packs a powerful punch, because it's a great reminder of the humanity of Jesus.

It's often easy to picture Jesus as the babe in the manager and then — blink, blink — as a fully-grown man, as if those were the only two distinctive phases of His human, physical form. That's what we see in art — a baby in the manager, usually smiling and happy; or a fully grown European-looking man with long hair, blue eyes, and a nicely trimmed beard.

But as a human, Jesus did what all of us do as humans: He changed physically. His feet got bigger, His arms longer, His face went from that of a baby, to that of a toddler, to that of a pre-teen, to that of a teen (did He have pimples?), and, eventually, to that of a grown man, probably not with blue eyes but most likely with a beard.

I wonder sometimes about the physical appearance of Jesus. How tall was He? How long was His hair? Was His beard short or long, full or scraggly? Was He thin? Did He have washboard abs? Did He develop big biceps from all that work as a carpenter before He started preaching?

Based upon what's known of the people of His day, the region, and His ancestry, we could speculate that Jesus was about 5-foot-2 with dark wavy or curly hair and olive-colored skin. But look around you: If someone 2,000 years from now used only what they knew of the people of our time and place in history to come up with a description of your appearance, how close would they get?

We know from the Bible that we are all equal in eyes of God, but we know from observation that He created us in unique shapes, forms, sizes, and looks — especially in America.

We are shaped to some degree by our heredity and ethnicity, but that, in our melting pot nation, can be misleading. I grew up in, and still live in, Arkansas. What picture does that bring to mind for you? A hillbilly? A farmer in the Delta? Bill Clinton? Do you picture me as black, white, Hispanic, Native American? Tall, short, thin, chubby?

When I look at my father, his father, and his father's father, I see a line of relatively tall, relatively thin men.

Of course, my dad married a woman whose ancestors were mostly Dutch and mostly on the short side, and my mom's genes won out when God created me. My dad was a solid six-one, but I'm barely five-ten (and somehow getting shorter every year, it seems).

Even among nationalities we see tremendous diversity. The tallest person who ever lived, at least that we know of, was Robert Wadlow, an American who stood eight feet, eleven inches and was still growing until his death at the all-too-young age of 22. If you look on Wikipedia for a list of the tallest men, however, you'll find that the top 20 includes someone from just about every region of the world — the U.S., Germany, China, Indonesia, France, Libya, Mozambique, Iran, Morocco, Ireland, Turkey, Canada, Finland, Ukraine. But you'll also find many of the same countries represented on the list's shortest people.

So while it's easy to describe the "typical" person of any time and place, it's a bit like sticking one hand in boiling water and the other in a freezer saying that, on average, you feel quite nice.

The Bible, perhaps to allow us each to see God's Son in a way that's personally approachable and comforting to each of us, doesn't speak directly about the appearance of Jesus as a child or as an adult.

Isaiah, describing Jesus as the suffering servant, says, "He had no beauty or majesty to attract us to Him, nothing in His appearance that we should desire Him." *(Isaiah 53:2)* Is that metaphorical? Is it describing Jesus at the time of His persecution and death? Or is it a general statement of how He looked when He was on earth? Is it saying Jesus was, well, somewhat homely?

One dictionary defines the Greek word for *stature* that's used in Luke 2:52 as "height and comeliness of stature," which would indicate Jesus was a good-looking fellow. And clearly there were times during His ministry when people were drawn to Him. Was there some sort of divine charisma, a part of His special anointing that allowed others a mystical insight into His divinity? Or was He just a nice-looking fellow?

Homely or comely? Both? Neither? And does it matter?

It most likely mattered in some way or another to those who saw and knew Jesus when He was alive, but it hardly matters now. Jesus was and is the Son of God. Jesus is God. That's what really matters.

On the other hand, knowing that God became man, fully human, and saw His body change with the passing of time, not to mention with the inflictions of mankind's punishment, is both interesting and insightful. He felt the cool of a breeze, the sting of the cold, the warmth of His mother's touch, and, of course, the pain of His tormentor's whip.

Throughout Scripture, we see that God cares about our physical health and that Jesus cared about His health and the health of others. Jesus didn't worship His body and, ultimately, He sacrificed it for the sake of humanity and in obedience to God. But His obedience to the Father also leads us to a bigger principle that, while not explicitly stated in Luke 2:52, is supported by the whole of Scripture: Jesus took care of His body so we should, too.

Many of us don't, of course. We spend a disproportionate amount of our time, energy, and income to feed our ego, our pride, and our selfish desires rather than taking care of our bodies.

We don't have the time to exercise, but we have time to watch a three-hour movie while eating buttered popcorn and drinking a sugar-filled soft drink.

We don't have the money for "whole foods," but we spend lavishly on luxury items like cars or even daily purchases like sugar-filled coffee.

What's wrong with all of that? God has blessed us in America with so much. Why not eat, drink, and be merry, for, as the saying goes, tomorrow we may die? Isn't this the American Dream?

Like any question, we can find the answer by asking and answering either of the following: Is it Biblical? Does it bring glory to God?

Clearly God wants us to take care of our bodies — not because He's a nagging God who wants to "make" us eat our broccoli and kale, but because He loves us and wants what's best for us. Why is taking care of our bodies best for us and how does it bring glory to God?

For starters, our body is the home of the Holy Spirit. 1 Corinthians 6:19-20 says, "Do you not know that your bodies are temples of the Holy Spirit, who is in you, whom you have received from God? You are not your own; you were bought at a price. Therefore honor God with your bodies."

We should give God a nice place to live, don't you think? When we get to heaven, God tells us, we'll get a new body, so apparently He wants us to have a strong, healthy body. That's part of His design for us. He makes all things right. God made our bodies, and we can honor Him by taking care of them in this sin-stained state until He makes them new and right again.

Jimmy Peña, the founder of Prayfit, points out that God's grace gives us the freedom to accept ourselves as we are, wrinkles and all, and the obligation to take care of ourselves the best we can.

"Grace removes the burden of trying to perfect a body that won't last, and yet grace is the reason to honor it, every day that it does," Peña told the authors of *The Daniel Plan*. "It's not about the mirror; it's about the One we are trying to mirror."

The second reason taking care of our bodies is good for us and honoring to God involves the connection between our bodies, our minds, and our spiritual life.

Sin typically begins in our thought lives. When our thoughts drift to unhealthy places, we make decisions that are unhealthy — with the words we say or don't say to others and the actions we take or don't take. When our thoughts are pure and healthy, we make healthy, pure decisions. When our thoughts are on God, we make Godly decisions and take godly actions. We speak and act with spiritual courage. We listen to God and live accordingly.

The Apostle Paul put it this way, "Finally, brothers and sisters, whatever is true, whatever is noble, whatever is right, whatever is pure, whatever is lovely, whatever is admirable — if anything is excellent or praiseworthy — think about such things." *(Philippians 4:8)*

One important but often-neglected way of keeping our minds healthy and pure is to keep our bodies healthy and pure. Romans 12:1-2 tells us to "...give your bodies to God...Let them be a living and holy sacrifice — the kind He will find acceptable. This is truly the way to worship Him. Don't copy the behavior and customs of this world, but let God transform you into a new person by changing the way you think." *(NLT)* Or, as other versions put it, we are "transformed by the renewing of our mind." *(NIV)*

Not only does our mind affect our body, but our body affects our mind. Rick Warren says, "What you do with your body sets the tone for everything else." Why? Because the food we eat contributes to the chemical makeup of our bodies. When we eat a healthy diet and keep our bodies fit through exercise, we become more emotionally and mentally healthy.

Personally, a healthy diet has dramatically reduced some of the digestive issues I had experienced for years. The biggest physical benefit for my wife has been fewer headaches. And because we're more rested and physically healthy, we're better equipped spiritually, emotionally, and mentally to do the things God calls us to do.

I like this summation from Warren's book, *The Daniel Plan*: "If you nourish your body with high-quality ingredients from real food, not only will you increase your energy, lose weight, and reverse many chronic illnesses, but you will also feel lighter and more motivated to exercise, your mood will lift, and your brain will have better clarity, allowing you to clear out the debris in the way of your relationships with others and God."

This is the *right* reason for taking care of your body — to bring glory to God. There are, of course, *wrong* reasons to get fit and healthy. Comedian and social critic George Carlin once joked "America has lost its soul; now it's trying to save its body." I suspect he had no idea how true that statement was, much less how the two ideas were actually tied together. People who are lost spiritually turn to many different things in search of a god, and one of those things is *self*. So many of the people who spend hours each week in the gym are sculpting their bodies for the wrong reason — vanity, not godliness.

It's amazing, but not surprising, that America has been in a "fitness craze" for nearly 50 years, and, yet, the nation as a whole is less healthy. Mark Hyman, one of the co-authors of *The Daniel Plan*, points out one reason for this: "You can't exercise your way out of a bad diet." So if you want to get healthy physically, you need a combination of diet and exercise. But real wellness takes you somewhere deeper — somewhere you can only go with Jesus. That's because spiritual health and physical health are interwoven. Physical health promotes spiritual well-being, but physical health without a focus on God is nothing more than idolatry.

For Jesus to grow in wisdom, He needed to take care of His physical body. For Jesus to grow in favor with God and man, He needed to take care of His physical body. And for us to grow like Jesus, we need to take care of our physical bodies as we fix our eyes on Jesus.

Go Forth and Grow It

The scale is a liar.

There, I said it. That relatively small machine that blinks numbers at me each Saturday morning has an agenda, and it's to bring me down.

OK, maybe that's a bit extreme. Maybe the scale is a machine without malice. Maybe I just added a pound or two last week. Maybe I should have exercised more; and by "more" I mean "some." Maybe I should have eaten fewer of those dark chocolate almonds. Maybe I should ask God to help me do better this week and not worry about where I failed last week.

Questions

- How does the humanity of Jesus shape your view of Him?

- How much time to you spend on things that impact your health in a positive way? Consider these tasks: Planning meals, shopping for the right foods, cooking, exercising, and sleeping.

- Reflect on 1 Corinthians 6:19-20 — "Do you not know that your bodies are temples of the Holy Spirit, who is in you, whom you have received from God? You are not your own; you were bought at a price. Therefore honor God with your bodies." What impact does this verse have on your view of your self-image? How will your view of this verse shape your thoughts, words, and actions?

- Describe how you have experienced the connections between your body, mind, and spiritual life?

- How does the way you care for your body bring glory to God?

- Do you ever find yourself placing your physical health and appearance as an idol that takes your focus away from fully honoring the Lord? Conversely, do you feel your lack of attention to good fitness and diet habits might cause you to feel sluggish and hinder your ability to give attention to your time with the Lord?

- How does vanity shape your view of yourself and God? What triggers you to see yourself at one extreme or the other — either obsessing about how "good" you look or lamenting that you don't look way you want to look? And how does that shape your emotional and spiritual outlooks?

- Who is one fellow follower of Christ in your life (of your gender) who you feel gives proper attention to their personal health, without idolizing it? Can you contact that person about praying with you as you seek to better honor God with your body?

- How can you impact the health of the people you care about in ways that are responsible and respectful? (Your spouse, your children, your friends, your co-workers?)

Go-Do's

Consider these sources for growing in stature and come up with ways you can tap into them more regularly:

Pray: Boldly pray to God about your wellness. The Holy Spirit resides in your body, so seek His guidance through prayer. Ask God to strengthen your will and to help you have the discipline to do or not do the things that will lead to greater physical, mental, spiritual, and emotional wellness. Seek forgiveness when you come up short of your goals, and embrace the grace that God provides. Remember, God is more concerned with the condition of your heart than the size of your waistline.

Read: Start with the Word of God. Intentionally read and reflect on passages that speak to God's view of your physical body and how you take care of it. What does it mean to be made in His image? What does His word say about worshiping Him through the way you take care of yourself? With a Biblical perspective and foundation, consider other sources to help guide your approach to fitness. There's an overload of information, so vet the source and keep an open mind.

Listen: Everyone has an opinion on what it means to take care of your body, and it makes sense to keep an open mind. But listen to what God is telling you through the Biblically grounded sources you most respect and trust. One of those sources is your body. As you make changes, listen to your body. What changes help you feel better and bring you closer to God?

Act: Put what you're learning into action. Go on a walk. Join a gym. Tell the waiter not to bring the rolls. Go to bed at a regular time each night with a goal of sleeping 7-8 hours. Practice cooking healthy meals. Take a class on it. Consider going on a 40-day fast that limits what you put in your body. Use the time to pray and draw closer to God, but also to cleanse your body of the bad stuff you've been putting into it for so many years. Then add things back in intentional ways so you can feel how different foods affect your moods and how you feel.

CHAPTER 5
FAVOR WITH GOD

"My grace is sufficient for thee. The words soothed her soul like a healing balm."

An Unforgivable Secret, J.E.B. Spredemann

My wife and I enjoy spending time together, and we enjoy traveling to new places and seeing new things. So on the flight home from our honeymoon in Mexico, we began a list of places we'd like to visit if time, finances, and, most importantly, God would allow.

Then we began saving, planning and, eventually, going. Some of these trips were weekend getaways, some were "normal" vacations, and some were special trips that were years in the making.

We haven't gone through the list, but we've made progress and even hit a few spots that weren't on it originally. In pretty quick fashion, Mexico was followed by Denver, Phoenix, Dallas, Memphis, Hot Springs, Ark., the Outer Banks of North Carolina, Haiti, Branson, Mo., San Francisco, Kansas City, Williamsburg, N.C., Italy, and New York City.

In some cases, the vacation piggybacked on a work trip (Denver and New York) or a family wedding (Williamsburg). One trip (the Outer Banks) was a vacation with my extended family but also the front end of a mission trip we made to Haiti.

In every case, however, we pray about the trips and plan for the trips. For instance, it took us three-and-a-half years to save for the trip to Italy and several months to plan it. I give my wife all the credit on this. We aren't wealthy by American standards, but she is fantastic at saving money and at planning trips that are cost-effective but that don't put us in roach motels.

In short, we've been blessed to travel to some interesting places.

In fact, we've been blessed in lots of areas of life.

Consider our home. We live in a modern, two-story brick home with picturesque views from our lot near the top of a hill. We can look out over town from a four-level deck. In the winter, when the leaves are off the trees, we can see for miles. In the summer, when fireworks are going off to celebrate the Fourth of July, we can see all the shows from the comfort of home as they explode above the tree lines. We live only a few minutes from work and shopping, but we're removed enough that hardly a day goes by when we don't see a deer on or near our property.

And there are our vehicles. I drive a four-door Tundra, and my wife drives a Cadillac.

And our work. We both have good jobs working with people we like and doing things we believe will make the world a better place.

And our health. It's good.

And our family. Between us, we have seven children and, at last count, 12 grandchildren. Defying the odds, all of them are smart and beautiful!

Best of all, there's our marriage. I love my wife. I try my best to treat her like a queen, not because I have to or because she pressures me, but because I love her more than anything. Taking care of her just feels right. It's fulfilling. One of the songs I sing to her most often is the Al Green classic *Let's Stay Together*: "I...I'm so in love with you. Whatever you want to do...is alright with me-e-e-e-e." She's perfect for me. She satisfies me in every way. Physically, emotionally, and spiritually, she makes me a better man.

And there you have it. My life, if you wanted to look at it a certain way, is a great big advertisement for the "Prosperity Gospel." You know: God loves you and wants what's best for you, so He'll give you whatever you ask for. Just ask. Name it and claim it.

There's just one problem with that: It's not true.

All the evidences I described of our blessings are true, but we never named them and claimed them. And I painted only one piece of our life for you. I omitted quite a few details along the way. Through selective omission, I left out the pain and heartache Audrey and I each experienced before we met. I ignored the challenges we face each day. I conveniently skipped over the struggles of our children and grandchildren, the times when the relationships with our children are strained. I didn't mention the times when my work is downright painful — when clients are unfairly demanding or when writing one simple sentence seems harder than bringing peace to the Middle East. Or when Audrey's work is challenging – when some of the students in her classes are making poor behavior choices or when the bureaucracy of a large school district makes progress feel like a rock in the mud.

Jesus said, "In this world you will have trouble," (*John 16:33*) and, of course, we do. Life is great, but it's not perfect. I could give you a long list of the imperfections. Some of them, you could spot easily enough just by getting to know us a little. You would see the results of my sinfulness, of what happens because of my pride, my selfishness, my passiveness, my defensive nature, my stubbornness, my tendency to either avoid confrontation or to blow up like a stick of dynamite in a campfire. Others are harder to see. But they are there. Trust me. They are there.

At a casual glance, however, I suspect most of you would look at Audrey and me and say something like, "There's a couple that's doing well. God is blessing them."

And we'd agree. But how do you really know?

All the "life is great" stuff in our life might be an indication that God is blessing us. Or, frankly, it might not be. Did God give me a nice (used, by the way) truck as a blessing or was it a selfish purchase born of my sin nature? You can't answer, because you don't know the condition of my heart. Even the fruit of my good works can deceive you. What's on the surface (or the branches) tells you something, but not everything you really need to know to answer the question.

What at first glance seems simple and straightforward is, with closer inspection, nuanced and complex. And that's the challenge with this part of our verse: It looks so simple and easy and obvious, but it's really not.

Jesus grew...in favor with God.

What's that mean? It's simple. He made God happy, right? God looked at what Jesus was doing, and He smiled. Well, maybe. Possibly. Partly. But I believe there's more.

***

Sometimes I've found myself listening to a sermon and the pastor will take a word from the Scripture and provide the definition from the original language. That's typically very helpful, but there are also those times when the definition will stray so far from the English word that it's a bit confusing. It's like he's saying, "Your translation says *chair* but in the Greek it really means *spoon*."

The word *favor* doesn't go that far, but, if you're like me, you may have to connect the etymological dots to understand it a little better. We usually think of *favor* in two ways — as an attitude of approval (that was a favorable result) or as an act of kindness (she did us a huge favor). It comes from the Greek word *charis*, which is defined as "grace, as a gift of blessing brought to man by Jesus Christ; favor; gratitude; thanks; a favor or kindness." *(Strong's Concordance)*

So is it the same to say Jesus grew in "grace" with God as it is to say He grew in "favor" with God? Some translations actually word it that way.

The conflict, for me at least, is this: When I *grow* in some area of life, that indicates that I'm getting better in that area, which means it's something I do, something I work for, something I earn. In fact, when I searched the Internet one morning for "favor with God," several of the top results were blogs or articles with titles along the lines of "How to get and keep God's favor." Grace, on the other hand, is something I can't earn. But that's not what the verse is suggesting.

First, a short reminder: The ultimate grace of God is His gift of salvation to those who willingly accept it. If you believe in Jesus as the Son of God and that He is the only way to find cover for your sins, then you, through no work of your own, are saved from the consequences of your sins — death — and can experience eternal life with a perfect God.

That's grace. Amazing grace. A perfect God allowed His Son to die for our sins so that we can spend eternity with Him in heaven — and not get what we deserve, which is eternity separated from God, otherwise known as hell.

In other words, Jesus brings us into a right and eternal relationship with God.

And God is always more concerned with your relationship with Him than any outcome of your works. David English, a friend of mine who works for Campus Crusade, often puts it this way: "God cares more about *who you are* than *what you do.*"

Jesus, as God himself, always had and always will have a right relationship with God. It wasn't something he needed to grow. There were two events during the life of Jesus when people actually heard God say that Jesus is "my Son, whom I love; with Him I am well pleased."

One occurred when Jesus was baptized, *(Matthew 3:17, Mark 1:11, Luke 3:22)* the other was during the "transfiguration" described in Matthew 17:5, Mark 9:7, and Luke 9:35. So one was before Jesus accomplished anything with His earthly ministry, and the other was during His ministry but before the ultimate purpose had been accomplished. God's love for and pleasure with Jesus was unconditional.

As a man, however, Jesus somehow was able to grow in favor — or grace — with God.

That's because God's grace doesn't end with salvation. It's also a maintaining presence in our lives — the sustaining influence that allows us to mature as disciples of Christ. This is what the theologians call sanctification. It's that phase in our journey when the Holy Spirit works on our spiritual maturity by setting us "apart" for God's purposes. The Baptist Faith and Message says that it begins "in regeneration" and "growth in grace should continue throughout the regenerated person's life." This is not only how we grow *like* Jesus, but how we grow to *be like* Jesus.

So we are saved by grace alone, and by His grace we act obediently, and as we act obediently we grow in His grace. Thus, this type of grace — this favor — speaks partly, perhaps largely, to our obedience to God. Unlike us, Jesus never disobeyed God. But like us, each act of obedience He took allowed Him to grow in favor with

God. (Notice that the verse says He grew "in" favor; it doesn't say He grew "His" favor; God didn't and couldn't love Him more.)

When we act in obedience to God's call on our lives, God is pleased with us. He's like a parent who sees his child acting rightly. He celebrates it for us and with us. There's an increase in intimacy, not because God loves us more when we act in obedience but because our obedience can't be accomplished if we're not dependent upon the Holy Spirit. Thus, obedience brings us closer to God.

When we're closer to God, we're walking in faith. We're trusting Him. We're bringing Him glory. We're acting as He would have us act. We're experiencing God. And that pleases God, because He wants what's best for us.

When we disobey God, our relationship (as believers) doesn't change, but we, by our own actions, cause breaks in our fellowship with God. We are trusting in ourselves, not God. We aren't walking in faith or dependence. God is there, but we aren't listening to Him, we aren't holding closely to Him, we aren't experiencing Him. And this saddens God, because, again, He wants what's best for us.

So for me, this might be the most fundamentally important question we can ask each day: Is God pleased with the way I'm living my life?

Is He pleased with my thought life? Is He pleased with the way I speak to my wife? Is He pleased with how I invest my time? Is He pleased with my work? Is He pleased with how I'm using the money He's given me? On and on it can go.

It's worth repeating that God loves us for *who we are* not *what we do*, so we can't ask those questions in a way that leads us on a path to a works-driven theology. But that doesn't mean we shouldn't make an effort to please the God we love. My hope and prayer isn't for perfection here on earth, but for progress toward perfection. I want to grow in favor with God.

And how will I know if that's happening?

The blessing of the favor, or grace, of God takes many forms, some of which look like blessings to the world around us and some of which look like peace in the midst of trouble.

Theologian Alexander MacLaren (1826-1910) once made an interesting connection between grace, mercy, and peace as blessings that flow "from the fountain head" and slowly work their way down to a "lodgment in the heart of man." Grace, he said, is a "Divine attitude or thought," mercy, the "manifestation of grace in act[ion]," and peace the "issue of the soul."

"These three come down, as it were, a great, solemn, marble staircase from the heights of the Divine mind, one step at a time, down to the level of earth; and the blessings which are shed along the earth," MacLaren wrote in *Expositions Of Holy Scripture*. "Such is the order. All begins with grace; and the end and purpose of grace, when it flashes into deed, and becomes mercy, is to fill my soul with quiet repose, and shed across all the turbulent sea of human love a great calm, a beam of sunshine that gilds, and miraculously stills while it gilds the waves."

In some of the worst times of my life, I've felt the grace, mercy, and peace of God because I felt His presence while dealing with the difficult circumstances.

In fact, during the absolute worst period in my life, I fell on my knees before God in total surrender like never before. I committed to releasing all the troubles of my first marriage to Him in a very new and more consistent way. By His grace, I was able to live that more consistently, but the results weren't what I expected. I did my best to accept responsibility for all the things I did to cause problems in the marriage, I did my best to act in obedience to God in each moment, I did my best to accept His forgiveness when I failed, and I did my best to trust Him for the results. And guess what happened? The situation actually got worse. But I grew closer to God. I trusted Him even more. I *felt* His favor. It was incredibly freeing.

Then the situation ended, not with the outcome I thought God would bring about, but in divorce. God hates divorce, right? I was a bit confused. I battled feelings of failure, and I would have given myself over to them except for one thing — I knew in my heart that I had been trusting God for the results.

So, with God's help, I just kept trusting Him.

As I went through this crucible period, I wasn't sure what was next. Frankly, I expected to spend the rest of my life alone (unmarried), even though my heart longed for a Godly woman to share life and faith with. I felt I was created for intimacy with another person — it can be part of how God allows us to experience intimacy with Him — but I'd never had that and believed I probably never would. I'd have to wait for heaven.

All of my experiences, however, somehow prepared me for what happened next. I believe I was growing in favor with God, and, by His mercy, He led me to the most perfect woman in the world for me. God provided an incredible, trusting, loving relationship, and my relationship with God grew deeper and more meaningful.

I know divorce is a touchy and somewhat contentious topic among followers of Jesus, so I want to make my view on it clear: God didn't cause my divorce, but He sustained me through it and provided me with opportunities to grow from it. I believe if two followers of Jesus trust God for their marriage, then He will help them work through any problems and challenges they face. And I believe there are times when God calls someone to stay in a difficult marriage for reasons we can't fully understand. On the other hand, there also are extreme situations when God clearly allows one of His followers to leave a marriage.

If you're in a difficult marriage, my simple advice is this: Seek qualified, Bible-believing counsel; don't rush down the easy, selfish road; and trust and honor God at all costs.

If we want to grow in favor with God, I believe it's essential to trust God regardless of the situation. My example is relational, but it could just as easily be financial, work-related, or in some other area of your life. You might have to trust God to see you through the death of a loved one, the loss of a job, the disappointment of a child's choices in life, of a natural disaster that's destroyed your possessions. Or you might have to trust Him with something the world sees as a positive — the birth of a child, a promotion at work, recognition from others, a marriage to a person who fits you perfectly.

As humans, we can't always discern what God causes versus what God allows, but we know God is in control. We know if we trust Him for the results, He will get the glory and we will get what's best for us. But that won't look the same for everyone. It might be a long struggle with illness. It might be a life of persecution that ends in martyrdom. It might be a life of service as a missionary in a foreign land. Or it might be the life of a CEO who helps fund that missionary.

I've heard it said that God cares more about our holiness than our happiness, and I believe that to be true. So here's what I ultimately believe about growing in God's favor: It's not about the results, it's about the faith.

If we're walking in faith and obedience to God, we don't worry about the results. We may not have enough money for the rent or to fix the leaky plumbing. We may feel stuck in a marriage that's devoid of trust and intimacy. Or we may have a nice house and a great marriage, and we may get to go to Italy on vacation. Regardless, we're responsible for our actions that helped create those situations, and we're responsible for whether we approach them selfishly or with faith and trust in God. And it's only when we're walking in faith that we will grow in God's favor.

Go Forth and Grow It

Keeping God top-of-mind during the everyday moments of life can prove difficult. It's easy to find ourselves in a conversation with someone, for instance, and realize that they've hurt our feelings in a small way. It probably wasn't intentional, and it wasn't a big deal, but it leads to a coarse word in response. That leads to more hurt feelings, and the next thing we know neither of us are honoring God. Neither of us are making God happy.

Neither of us are growing in God's favor. We didn't even see the slippery slope; then we blinked and found ourselves in a high-speed free-fall.

It's more natural to turn to God when things are at the extremes — when disaster strikes we fall to our knees in desperation and call out to God for help; or when something amazingly wonderful happens, we lift our hands in joyful thanksgiving.

Growing in favor with God is about developing a more consistent intimacy with Him until that day when he completes us. Until then, we're all a work in progress. But we're in the hands of a master builder.

Questions

- What do you believe about Jesus? To fully experience God's grace, you have to first settle the question of how you view God's Son. Do you believe Jesus is the Son of God and the only way to find cover for your sins? If so, what is your response to that amazing grace?

- How would you describe God's grace to you for your salvation?

- How would you describe God's grace as a sustaining influence in your life?

- What might others around you see in your life as evidence that you are growing in favor with

God? Is that an accurate reflection of your relationship with the Lord?

- Spend five minutes reflecting on a time when disobedience to God caused a break in your fellowship with God. Then spend five minutes reflecting on a time when obedience to God drew you closer to God. What lessons can you learn from those reflections? How have you felt the grace, mercy, and peace of God in your life?

- How are you allowing the Holy Spirit to impact the critical areas of your life: your thought life, your words, your time, and your actions? Consider how these are impacting things like your finances, your family relationships, your work relationships, your friendships, your community, and the broader world.

- What might be hindering your intimacy with the Lord? What steps can you take to free yourself from those hindrances?

Go-Do's

Consider these ways for growing in favor with God and come up with ways you can tap into them more regularly:

Pray: Ask God to search your heart and open your mind to your sinfulness. Confess those sins and give them to God. Ask boldly for God to work in you and through you so that you can "go and sin no more," and thank Him in advance for His answers to your prayers. Speak to Him in desperation. Your life's circumstances might not seem desperate, but your need for God's favor is.

Read: Once again, start with God's word. In addition to the verses referenced in this chapter, consider reading 1 Chronicles 4:10 and Bruce Wilkinson's book, *The Prayer of Jabez*. As you read books and articles that speak to God's blessings, remember to filter them through the whole of Scripture. This is a topic where many authors take Scripture out of context to promote ideas and philosophies that don't align with the entirety of God's teachings.

Listen: God is in the whisper. Listen for His response to you. Often, the act of stilling and quieting ourselves is what brings us closer to God and allows us to connect with Him in deeper obedience.

Act: Obedience is difficult. We are born with a sin nature that drives us toward selfish behaviors. We want immediate gratification rather than trusting that doing the right thing brings better results over time. So commit to doing the next right thing, even if it's not the easiest thing.

CHAPTER 6
FAVOR WITH MAN

*"When you stop expecting people to be perfect,
you can like them for who they are."*

Donald Miller

In the 1930s, a relatively obscure guy living in New York City wrote what started out as a textbook for the classes he taught to adults on public speaking and human relationships. During the Great Depression era, this book offered some much-needed insights, principles, skills, and techniques that promoted individual success.

How to Win Friends & Influence People by Dale Carnegie became one of the best-selling business books of all time and spawned a cottage industry that still thrives. Millions of copies have influenced tens of millions of people, including my friend Tommy Spaulding.

Tommy and I met when he was writing his first book, *It's Not Just Who You Know* — a best seller in its own right, although not (yet) to the scale of Carnegie's. Tommy asked me to help him write his book, which is the type of project that often turns friends into enemies. Instead, it turned strangers into the best of friends.

If you knew Tommy, you wouldn't be surprised.

Tommy grew up in Suffern, N.Y., in a pretty stereotypical middle class environment. His parents weren't poor but neither did they have much money for the non-essentials of life. It wasn't a lack of money, however, that put up the greatest obstacle to Tommy's success. Instead, what really threatened to push Tommy down was his learning disability.

Tommy was in college before his disability was correctly diagnosed as dyslexia, and not much was known about it at the time. All through school, he just knew he wasn't like most of the other kids when it came to reading. It was tough to deal with — emotionally and academically. But unlike so many children who struggle with learning disabilities, Tommy became determined not to let that hold him back. He found ways to overcome that disability, and the more he overcame it the stronger he became in the belief that he could overcome it at any time and in any situation.

That didn't happen without some help, of course.

Tommy's dad, a school principal, looked at his son and saw potential, but he wasn't blind to the challenges Tommy faced. "Son, your mother is going to insist that you read one book — the Bible," Tommy's dad said. "And

I'm going to ask that you read this one." Then he gave Tommy a copy of Dale Carnegie's *How to Win Friends & Influence People.*

Reading that book had to have been terribly hard for Tommy, but he did it. And then he lived it. Tommy moved forward in life because of his unmatched optimism, his unquestionable work ethic, and his incredible ability to practice what he learned from Carnegie's book about developing relationships.

By the time Tommy and I met, he was nearly 40 years old and he had earned two Master's degrees, traveled to dozens of countries, been the CEO of a large, respected non-profit organization, and built a reputation as a dynamic public speaker.

"I not only learned the art of winning friends and influencing people, but of *mastering* relationships, personally and professionally," Tommy explains in the intro to his book.

Tommy took Carnegie's message, lived it to the full, and experienced incredible worldly success along the way. But he also realized that valuing relationships isn't enough — you have to value people. And Tommy values people.

"I began digging much deeper into the value of great relationships and the ways to go about developing them," he wrote. "Carnegie's principles and techniques seem timeless. And most are. That's why his book has sold more than 15 million copies. But it's time to broaden the scope and influence that were central to his message."

Tommy's book achieved that goal. It describes the value of powerful relationships — Fifth Floor Relationships, as Tommy calls them — and how to pursue them in everyday life, not just with a few people. These are relationships that value people, selflessness, and ideals rooted in God's word. These relationships move beyond the transactional (First Floor) to the transformational (Fifth Floor).

Here's how Tommy puts it: "When I look back at how the power of relationships lifted me — a skinny kid with a lisp, below average grades, and a learning disability — out of a middle-class community and put me in leadership positions that took me all around the world, I can boil it down to this: It's not about me."

***

No one in the history of history valued transformational relationships more than Jesus. So when Luke 2:52 says that Jesus grew "in favor with...man," we see that His primary focus on His Father didn't come at the expense of His earthly brethren. It wasn't "God or people"; it was "God *and* people."

But once again we have to ask: What does it mean to "grow in favor" with people? It's similar to what we looked at in the previous chapter, except this time there's a twist. Remember, the definition of *favor* involved grace and gratitude. When Jesus grew in grace and gratitude with God, it showed up in the form of His obedience to God. When Jesus grew in grace and gratitude with people, it showed up in their obedience to Him. So when we grow in favor with people, it's with the hope of creating stronger relationships with Jesus — for others, but for us as well.

What did that look like for Jesus?

First, the good news: Each of us is able to have a deep, intimate, personal relationship with Jesus because, as His followers, the Holy Spirit lives within us. This is an incredible and powerful thing. But when Jesus walked on earth, He didn't have deep, intimate, and personal relationships with everyone He encountered. He loved everyone, but He didn't spend time with everyone. He didn't invest in every relationship equally. And some of His relationships were deeper and more personal than others.

Jesus preached to large crowds of people, many of whom never spoke with Him privately. He spoke with some people individually but only briefly. With someone like the woman at the well, you imagine a conversation that took only a few minutes. He had extended conversations and a more personal relationship with people like the family of Martha and Mary. He spent hours and hours over three years getting to know His disciples. And He spent even more time with Peter and John.

Likewise, God calls us to different types of relationships with different people.

I have a deep, intimate, and personal relationship with my wife. It's like no other relationship in my life, and that's the way it should be. As Genesis 2:24 puts it, "That is why a man leaves his father and mother and is united to his wife, and they become one flesh." I also have a few very close male friends. I have other friends who know me pretty well. And I have acquaintances — people who know me mainly on a surface level. Then I have the people I encounter along my path of life who only know of me by what they experience in that brief interaction.

All of those represent some type of relationship, and they all look different. I don't treat them all the same. There's a priority. No relationship, for instance, should ever drive a wedge between my wife and me. But in every relationship I hope that some how I'm honoring God and pointing the other person toward the King of kings.

**

Another observation about relationships from the life of Jesus is that while He loved everyone, everyone didn't love Him. The selflessness of Jesus didn't make Him a people-pleaser. He grew in favor with man, but not *all* men. He loved people enough to die for all mankind, but His love for people never took Him outside of God's will. That's a deeper, somewhat harder lesson in the way Jesus grew relationships; it's the lesson of tough love.

Jesus never backed off the truth because He was (and is) the Truth. He often won over the masses, but ticked off the established leaders. Some feared Him so much that they conspired to kill Him. That's not exactly showing their "favor," right?

Simply put, Jesus didn't grow in favor with people when it came at the expense of the truth.

At West Point, the military academy for the army, the cadets have a prayer that I first learned about in a book by my friend Mike Thompson (*The Anywhere Leader*). The prayer asks God for help doing the "harder right" over the "easier wrong." Jesus always did the harder right over the easier wrong, even if it made enemies instead of friends.

In today's world, Jesus might be seen as narrow-minded and intolerant, especially on issues like gay marriage or abortion. "He has strong beliefs and seems like a good person," people might say, "but He needs to learn to compromise more along the way. Sure He hangs out with people who are on the margins of society, but

He calls them sinners and asks them to repent. They've just chosen a different path to heaven, but Jesus wants to claim His way is the only way to heaven."

There are times when we need to practice the art of compromise, but not when it involves sacrificing the truth or denying Christ. As Jesus realized, the truth, even if we don't like it, is the only thing that truly sets us free. *(John 8:31-32)* He loved people so much that He always gave them the truth — the thing that was best for them — even when they didn't like it or didn't want it or didn't know that they needed it.

In the same way, Jesus never backed off of love, because Jesus *is* love. So even when He delivered a hard truth, He respected the humanity of the person. He spoke in parables. He asked questions that allowed people to self-discover answers. He offered indirect comments. He listened. And, at times, He spoke directly and plainly about things. His wisdom allowed Him to read each situation and provide what was needed, not just on the content of His words but in delivery of His message. There was love and compassion not only in His motives, but also in His actions. He spoke differently to rulers and religious experts than, say, to the woman at the well.

When we grow our relationships with other people, we have to be willing to take the risk of lovingly, compassionately sharing the hard truth with others — and listening to it with respect when they share it with us (even if they lack compassion).

That's not something that happens easily, especially when we haven't taken the time and invested the energy to really know someone. You've probably heard the expression, "People have to know you care before they'll care about what you know." That's not always true, but it's mostly true, especially when we're talking to non-believers about the Gospel of Christ.

All too often, we want to rush to the "truth" part and skip the "compassion" part. This is why "you'll burn in hell" evangelism so seldom works. We want to fix people, give them the solution, tell them what they need to know, because, dang it, *we know what they need to know!* And maybe we do. But if they immediately see us as narrow-minded, judgmental bigots, not as friends who love them, then we've effectively shut the door on ourselves.

My friend Walt Rakowich is great at relationship building, because he understands how to build trust with people. He has a pretty simple formula that's based on three core values — honesty, humility, and humanness, or what he calls a "3H-Core." When we are honest, humble, and value people for who they are as a creation of God, then we live in transparent, authentic, vulnerable ways that create trust. Without trust, relationships are shallow and powerless. With trust, relationships can grow and bloom.

Of course, even when we do everything well — as well as we humanly can — relationships often fall apart on us. We live in a fallen world filled with fallen people. We're each one of them. Mix sinful, prideful, selfish people into any setting, and it's amazing (that's grace) that any meaningful relationships ever develop.

Relationships, for most of us, are hard. They are even hard for my friend Tommy and people like him. They certainly are hard for me. I'm more of an introvert. I don't instinctively work toward transformational relationships. I don't have a natural charisma or an eloquent speaking style. I sometime stumble when trying to share my thoughts. And I typically don't do well in difficult conversations, because I'm not a big fan of criticism — at least not when it's directed at me. I can be defensive at times. Often, in fact. Challenge my actions or thinking and you know what you'll most likely hear, even if you're right? An excuse. I'll try to hide it in an explanation, but it's still an excuse. And I know that the closer I am to someone, the deeper the pain when the relationship feels stress. There's nothing worse for me than an argument with my wife, because there's no one on earth I love more.

Because I know all of this about myself, there are times when I'd prefer to live alone in a cave. No relationships, no conflicts.

Of course, that's not what God calls me — or any of us — to do. We're called to live in relationship with others — to grow in favor not just with God but also with people. It's within the framework of those relationships that people — us and others — grow in favor with God. For instance, when I work through conflict with my wife in a loving, healthy way, it always creates intimacy — between us, between me and God, and between us and God.

★★★

The Apostle Paul provides me with an unexpected example of how to grow in favor with man. Paul is known for many great things, but I had never thought of him as particularly strong when it comes to relationships. I always pictured Paul as blunt and a bit hardheaded.

Maybe he was, but it's clear that he valued relationships, especially with the churches he helped start during his missionary journeys. He wrote them often, expressed his love for them, and told them he wanted to see them again. And he didn't just do this when times were good.

At one point, Paul spent two years under house arrest in Rome, during which time he did some of his most important relationship building through the epistles (he wrote Ephesians, Colossians, and Philippians) and mentoring (Timothy, et al).

Paul valued relationships and put in the work to build and strengthen them, even during the most difficult of circumstances.

It takes work to do this type of relationship building. But here's the good news: We don't own the results. God owns the results.

No one in history was or is more misunderstood than Jesus. He was killed by those He came to save. He selflessly loved the world, and the world repaid Him by sentencing Him to an excruciating death nailed to a cross (preceded by all manner of beatings and other torture). If you or I had been around at the time — without knowing what we know today — we probably would have looked at the life of Jesus and said, "Well, that was good and all, but His ministry was hardly worth the price He paid. Look at the results: They killed Him."

But Jesus loved us enough to die for us because He trusted His Father with the results. When we grow in our relationships with other people, we aren't called to win them over or make them happy or give them what they want. We're called to follow Jesus. Speak the truth in love. Listen and learn from them. Help them. Serve them. Show mercy. Justice. Compassion.

God owns the results.

Again, this isn't easy. It involves investing in others. It involves transparency. It involves serving others. It involves trusting others. It involves accepting help from others. It involves forgiving others. And it involves releasing those results — willingly stepping back when we'd prefer to be in control.

Hard. Hard. Hard. Relationships are hard.

It seems to me, however, that God put this area of growth last on the list in Luke 2:52 *because* it's the hardest and *because* we need the others to accomplish it.

In other words, as we grow in Godly wisdom and as we mature physically and, most important, as we grow in our relationship with God, then we're in a position to bring God glory through our relationships with others — evangelism and discipleship, the Great Commission. We can step out of our comfort zones and trust God to use us in the world He created.

Go Forth and Grow It

Ah, yes, the Great Commission.

"Then Jesus came to them and said, 'All authority in heaven and on earth has been given to Me. Therefore go and make disciples of all nations, baptizing them in the name of the Father and of the Son and of the Holy Spirit, and teaching them to obey everything I have commanded you. And surely I am with you always, to the very end of the age.'" *(Matthew 28:18-20)*

Jesus came to seek and save the lost, but He left us with a role to play — to go make disciples. He didn't promise it would be easy, but He did promise to be with us as we "make disciples...baptize...and teach."

To play our role, we must build relationships. When people trust us and believe us, they begin to see Jesus as the reason for all that's good in our life. They see our weaknesses and how they are made strong through the living God. We become something God can use in some-one else's life. That's a powerful opportunity, and we all should take it, even if it comes with some challenges.

Questions

- Who do you know who is a selfless leader? Describe that person's attributes and actions, and consider ways you can emulate them.

- When has "tough love" from someone who cared about you produced positive results in your life?

- What situations cause you the most temptation to back away from God's truth when you find yourself in difficult conversations with people who aren't followers of Christ? How can you embrace compassion, empathy, and love without sacrificing truth?

- Relationships are two-way streets. How well do you listen to others and how can you improve when it comes to embracing the counsel of others?

- What are the three most amazing things that have happened in your life as a result of your relationship with Jesus that you can share with someone?

- What is the biggest factor preventing you from investing yourself in relationships with people around you? Business? Self-centeredness? Fear? Something else?

- Do you have a 3H-Core? How can you grow your reputation as someone who is honest, humble, and human?

- Who has God put around you? How might their lives and your relationship with each of them change if you begin investing more intentionally in the relationship?

Go-Do's

Consider these sources for growing in favor with people and come up with ways you can tap into them more regularly:

Pray: Ask God to identify the key relationships in your life you need to focus on and the areas within each relationship that needs your focus. Pray for ways to strengthen your core relationships (with your spouse, family, accountability partners) and to expand your relationships with people at work, in your community, and in those "divine appointments" with people you're meeting for the first time. Also ask God to give you the courage to speak when you should speak, the patience to listen when you should listen, the right words to say when you open your mouth, and to guide you in how you speak and listen to others.

Read: The Bible is full of stories about relationships between people, good and bad. As you read the Scriptures, pay attention to what it tells you about building powerful, strong, influential relationships. How did Paul relate to Timothy? What about Joseph and his brothers? What about Joseph and his unfair bosses or his ungrateful friends? What about Job and his friends? What about Ruth and her daughter-in-law? What about Daniel and the various kings of Babylon who ruled over him? What about Esther and Xerxes? What about Jesus and His disciples or the many people He encountered during His ministry?

Listen: Listen to the prompting of the Holy Spirit as it relates to your relationships. Also, seek the counsel of Godly family members and friends. If you've never taken a 360-degree assessment or a personality assessment, consider doing so and then listen to the results. These are tools that can help you develop greater self-awareness and others-awareness in your relationships. They can help you develop empathy for others so that you can speak with humility, transparency, compassion, and truth.

Act: There are two key action verbs in the Great Commission — go and make. Other verses in Scripture tell us to "be still" or to "wait," but here we find the God of the universe telling us to get off the couch and take action. We're like players on the teams that have made it to the Super Bowl — we've made it to the big game, we have a great plan, and we've been coached for success; now it's time to take the field. We're not cracking helmets with 300-pound linemen (thankfully); instead, we're looking to share the best news anyone we meet will ever hear.

CHAPTER 7
GROWING ONWARD

"Between the Bible and the Holy Spirit, you have everything you need to grow spiritually. And the more you grow, the more God can use you."

Elizabeth George

For many of us, the name "Clint Eastwood" brings to mind a half dozen or so of the most famous movie quotes ever written into a script. Even if you're so young that you've never heard of the former A-list, tough-guy actor, you likely know some of these famous lines he delivered:

"Go ahead...Make my day." (Dirty Harry)

"Do you feel lucky, punk? Well, do ya?" (Dirty Harry)

"When you hang a man, you better look at him." (Hang 'Em High)

"I'm not afraid of any man, but when it comes to sharing my feeling with a woman, my stomach turns to royal gelatin." (Every Which Way But Loose)

"Nothing wrong with shooting as long as the right people get shot!" (Magnum Force)

Perhaps my favorite Eastwood line shows up in the 1976 western, *The Outlaw Josey Wales,* when a bounty hunter confronts Wales (Eastwood) in a saloon:

"You're wanted, Wales," the bounty hunter says.

"Recon I'm right popular," Wales says. *"You a bounty hunter?"*

"A man's got to do something for a living these days," the bounty hunter explains.

Wales stares him down in classic Eastwood fashion and says, *"Dyin' ain't much of a living, boy."*

With those words, Eastwood expressed a cardinal rule for living: Don't die.

All of us, however, have this in common: We're dying.

Regardless of how healthy we keep our minds, bodies, and spirits, we're destined for another world, a world that follows death — heaven (eternity with God) or hell (eternity separated from God).

Our bodies have limitations, and physical death awaits us.

So, in light of that reality, a question also awaits us as we roll from the slumber of our beds each morning and into the challenges and blessings of a new day: How are we going to live while we're dying?

Early in life, the answer is instinctive because we're all about growth. We're growing up. We're experiencing all that life offers and learning to make our way in the world. We're making life happen. We're embracing the journey and all that comes with each new twist and turn.

Then something happens. That something is called *time*. We wake up one day and realize we're no longer getting taller, that life has settled into a bit of a routine, and that we see the world more like our parents.

"Eee-gad," we say, "I've gotten old! When did that happen?"

Life changes us and sometimes, like anything else that experiences some wear and tear, we lose a little of our shine.

The challenge as followers of Christ, of course, is to reinvent and reinvigorate — to grow like Jesus from the moment we embrace His call on our lives to the moment He calls us home.

Consider the life of Simon Peter. He was a fisherman who began following Jesus and became one of His disciples. Indeed, He was one of the disciples closest to Jesus and, at times, displayed great insight and faith.

When he first saw Jesus walking on water, for instance, Peter jumped out of the boat and went to meet Him. Then again, Peter took his eyes off Jesus and began to sink. "Lord, save me!" he cried out. Sound familiar?

It was also Peter who rashly cut off the ear of one of the men who had come to arrest Jesus. And it was Peter who denied Christ three times. Ultimately, however, Peter was a leader in the early church who lived for Jesus and gave his life for Him.

So we see in Peter a relatively common man with all the challenges common people face in life. He believed, but struggled with his belief. He acted rashly at times and had to be rebuked by Jesus. He showed great faith, but lost focus and made decisions that disappointed both himself and others. And still he is one of the models for how we can live out a vibrant faith in Christ.

Peter, like the rest of us, didn't wake up one day as the model Christian. He had to figure it out — just like me and just like you. Perhaps that's why Peter's parting advice to us is remarkably similar to Luke 2:52. At the end of his second letter, Peter tells us to "grow in the grace and knowledge of our Lord and Savior Jesus Christ." *(2 Peter 3:18)*

Peter issues this as a command — his final words — because he knows we have free will and can choose not to grow. And the opposite of growth isn't just death, it can be apostasy that leads to death. In fact, Peter sets up his final words with a warning to "be on your guard so that you may not be carried away by the error of the lawless and fall from your secure position." *(2 Peter 3:17)*

In his exposition of this passage, Alexander MacLaren says, "But remember dead things do not grow. You cannot grow unless you are alive, and you are not alive unless you have Jesus Christ."

As followers of Christ, we're called to stay connected to Christ — to stay alive in Christ by growing our faith in Jesus.

Nick Floyd, the teaching pastor at my church, sometimes quotes a model that describes the lifecycle of a typical church. I think it applies to individual followers of Jesus just as much as it applies to us as a collective group.

Nick says churches are born and typically go through four stages: Mission, ministry, maintenance, and monument.

In the beginning, they are driven by the call from God to do His work in a particular place at a particular time. That becomes their mission, and it's empowering and energizing.

There's a need and the church is meeting it, so they seek and attract the hurting and the lost, which means they must graduate to taking care of those people. That's ministry. This is rewarding but also difficult, draining, and challenging.

As time goes on and the church grows and matures, the focus shifts to maintenance — taking care of the people and the programs that resulted from the strong mission and the vibrant ministry. There's a tendency to take the foot off the gas and lock in the cruise control, if for no other reason than to catch a breath. Or, the church moves faster than ever, but only with the things (and people) that are right in front of them. They take pretty good care of their own, but there's no more growth.

With maintenance, routines set in and much of the attention shifts to what's *in the church* rather than what, and who, lives *outside the church* — a community and world that's still filled with lost and hurting people and a culture that's ever-changing. That's when the church becomes a monument — a stagnant pillar that people look at in admiration because of its notable past. It may inspire others at times, but it has no real future on its own and very little impact on the community it supposedly serves.

As individual followers of Jesus, we can fall into a similar lifecycle. We fall in love with Jesus and His glory becomes our mission, so we eat up all that anyone is willing to feed us about the God who saved us. We're eager to learn and grow.

This translates into service and sacrifice — ministry to others.

Then we need to catch our breath. The first breath or two rejuvenates us for more mission and ministry, but soon we find ourselves in maintenance mode. We may even become so busy with ministry that we no longer do anything to grow. We just work. Service becomes our idol.

And you know where we're going next: We're monuments to our past.

This isn't God's intention for us.

He has something more for us than rushing around chasing the next ministry opportunity until we fall over dead like the bounty hunter who confronted Josey Wales. And He also has something more for us than sitting on a rocking chair half asleep with drool spilling from the corners of our mouths as we mumble about the good old days.

That something is a journey of growth and intimacy that looks different for each of us.

It's true that from the moment we're born we begin the process of dying. But it's also true that we can keep growing until we're dead. Real growth takes place anytime we connect with God in an intimate way. That happens when we read the Bible. That happens when we pray. That happens when we sit still and listen for the Holy Spirit to stir within us. That happens when we look into the face of someone we're serving and see the pleasure of God. That happens when we're hurting and crying out to God. That happens when we're happy and shouting for joy.

Think of the best relationship you've ever known — parent to child, child to parent, friend to friend, husband to wife or wife to husband. When did you grow closer? During times of pain and struggle, you came together to face the challenges. During the routines of life, you walked together in simple appreciation. During the victories, you celebrated together.

You grew closer because you experienced life together.

Together.

That's what Jesus did. He experienced life with His Father.

And that's what He wants with us and for us. He wants us to experience life with Him.

That's what we can wake up each day in search of — intimacy with Jesus, intimacy with the Father. And that comes from daily drawing near to God and a daily commitment to growing like Jesus by experiencing life with Him.

So, what are you waiting on? Grow onward.

Go Forth and Grow It

Well, you've reached the end of this book, but certainly not the end of your journey. Here are a few final questions, but it's up to you to fill out the "Go-Do's."

Questions

- Think through each area in which Jesus grew. How might the ministry of Jesus been hindered if He had not grown in wisdom, in stature, in favor with God, and in favor with man?

- How can you imagine your ministry developing if you grow in the four areas and how might it be hindered if it doesn't?

- Look at Luke 2:52 one more time. What are your goals for your life in each of the four areas? What do you believe are God's goals for you in each area?

- What steps will you take with Him to chase those goals?

Go-Do's

Write a few sentences under each header to describe your next steps. You can write in this book or in a journal. Be specific and refer back to this at a set time each week:

Pray: _____

_____

_____

_____

_____

_____

_____

_____

_____

Read: _____

_____

_____

_____

_____

_____

_____

_____

_____

Listen: _____

_____

_____

_____

_____

_____

_____

_____

_____

_____

Act: _____

_____

_____

_____

_____

_____

_____

_____

_____

_____

A NOTE FROM THE AUTHOR

If you made it to this page, there's a good chance you read the book. Thanks! I hope you enjoyed it and found it helpful in your journey as a follower of Jesus. If so, please consider ways you can help spread the word so it might help others.

How?

Great question. Go to sites like Amazon.com and write a review. Talk about it on your social media sites like Facebook, Google-plus, and Twitter. If you have a blog, write a review about the book. If you're talking with friends and family, tell them about the book. If you know someone who might benefit from it, buy it for them as a gift. You get the idea. Spread the word.

Blessings,

Stephen Caldwell

AUTHOR BIO

Stephen Caldwell is the owner, chief word architect, and janitor of WordBuilders Communications. His career includes writing and editing credits in the newspaper, magazine, marketing, advertising, training, and book industries, and these days he spends most of his working hours either helping clients develop and share their ideas or wrestling with his own writing projects.

His work history includes journalism, an entrepreneurial effort as the executive editor of *The Life@Work Journal*, and four years as the director of learning experiences for SVI. Stephen and his wife, Audrey, are active in Cross Church of Fayetteville and in their community. They share a blended family that includes seven children and eleven (at last count) grandchildren. They enjoy spending time together however possible, but especially when it involves traveling or spoiling their grandkids.

APPENDIX 1

This isn't an exhaustive list of books, of course, but rather a few that I've found along the way that have helped me grow in wisdom and stature and in favor with God and man.

Celebration of Discipline by Richard J. Foster — Want to create spiritual depth? Sure you do! Foster's book is one of the best on what it looks like to do so.

Crazy Love by Francis Chan — The love of God is, well, crazy. It's bigger than we can imagine or understand. The only sane response to it, as Chan points out, is wholehearted devotion to Jesus.

It's Not Just Who You Know by Tommy Spaulding — A great book about the power of relationships at work.

Jesus Calling by Sarah Young — A terrific devotional book filled with short messages that will help you feel God's presence and peace.

Know What You Believe and *Know Why You Believe* by Paul E. Little — These two books have become classics for grounding our faith in the Word of God.

Knowing God by J.I. Packer — This isn't the easiest book in the world to read, but it's deep in theological truth about who God is and how we can relate to Him.

Mere Christianity by C. S. Lewis — This is considered one of the most important apologetic works on Christianity because it's darn good. It's one of those books you don't just read, but you re-read and re-read and re-read. Not because it's hard to understand but because it's just that good.

A Million Miles in a Thousand Years by Donald Miller — Pretty sure this isn't Miller's most commercially successful book, but I really like it because it's all about getting out there and living your story.

My Utmost for His Highest by Oswald Chambers — This classic book of devotionals will hit you hard with challenges to leave your comfort zone and walk more closely with God.

Ordering Your Private World by Gordon MacDonald — This is like sitting down with your loving but imperfect grandfather for some practical, easy-to-understand lessons on organizing your spiritual life.

Radical by David Platt — Don't read this if you want to hold fast to American materialism. Read it if you want to live in the truly radical way God calls us to live.

The Reasons for God by Tim Keller — Read anything by Tim Keller, but start with this one. It dismantles the arguments of those who would claim there is no God.

Tender Warrior by Stu Weber — This book is about what it means to be a man of God, so I mainly recommend it for men. As an aside, it's also a book God used to turn me from agnosticism. At some point in my reading, I put it down long enough to ask God to save me from my sins. So there's that.

The Circle Maker by Mark Batterson — This is an easy to read book that teaches you the power of persistent prayer.

The Daniel Plan by Rick Warren, Daniel Amen, and Mark Hyman — This book takes a holistic and Biblical approach to your health. It's not a fad diet. It's about a lifestyle. You have to make some radical changes to follow it, but you'll be shocked by the benefits.

The Purpose Driven Life by Rick Warren — This became a huge best seller for a reason: It's helpful. You read it and you learn stuff about your place in this universe and how to go about life as a follower of Jesus.

The Ragamuffin Gospel by Brennan Manning — As a fellow ragamuffin, I'm drawn to Manning's message on really living in God's grace.

The Return of the Prodigal Son by Henri Nouwen — This is a fascinating perspective on a parable most of us think we know. Nouwen uses Rembrandt's famous painting for a fresh look at this story of love and forgiveness.

THANKS

These people inspired me, encouraged me, and or advised me as I worked on this book: Jesus — my Lord; Audrey — my wife; Rebecca White, Ashley Brill, Andrew Caldwell, and Lauren Pickett — my children; Jackie West, Amanda Horton, and Josh Roy — Audrey's children; Austin, Madeline, Ella, Simeon, Paulina, Anna, Carson, Hudson, Landry, Madison, Abigail, and (TBD) — our grandchildren; Phil McMichael, Clif Anderson, Noe Garcia, and Nick Floyd — a few of our pastors; Robert Cupp, Michael Brown, Steve Beirise, Dave Flynn, David Jackson, and Alan Wagner — some of my friends; Mark Russell, Anna McHargue, Dave Troesh, Bobby Kuber, Todd Carman, and Emily Border — the team at Elevate Publishing; everyone who purchases this book; and anyone who reads it.

elevate
publishing

A strategic publisher empowering authors to strengthen their brand.

NO TREES WERE HARMED
IN THE MAKING OF THIS BOOK

OK, so a few did need to make
the ultimate sacrifice.

In order to steward our environment,
we are partnering with *Plant With Purpose*, to plant
a tree for every tree that paid the price for the printing of
this book.

PLANT W TH PURPOSE

www.plantwithpurpose.org

go to www.elevatepub.com/about to learn more

CPSIA information can be obtained at www.ICGtesting.com
Printed in the USA
BVOW02s1926040416

442928BV00004B/10/P

9 781943 425204